Rain Falling on Tamarind Trees

A Travelogue of Vietnam

C. L. Hoang

Willow Stream Publishing
San Diego

Rain Falling on Tamarind Trees
by C. L. Hoang

Copyright © 2018 Chinh L. Hoang

Published in the United States by Willow Stream Publishing
willowstreampublishing@gmail.com

ISBN: 978-0-9899756-0-5

Library of Congress Control Number: 2017912453

Cover Design and Interior Layout: Nick Zelinger

Some names and identifying details have been changed to protect the privacy of individuals.

First Edition

Printed in the United States of America

In loving memory of my parents

And

For all the people to whom Việt-Nam
means something

By C. L. Hoàng

Fiction
Once upon a Mulberry Field

Nonfiction
Rain Falling on Tamarind Trees

Contents

All around me: sky, mountains, and blue sea
Alone am I with my secret yearnings

—A 19th century poetess known as Bà Huyện Thanh-Quan
as she crossed over a mountain pass from northern to central Việt-Nam

Preface

By nature I am a slow planner, especially when it comes to long trips away from home. So imagine my surprise when in 2016 I was presented with an opportunity to join a group tour to Southeast Asia, with the main focus on Việt-Nam, and I heard myself spontaneously blurt out, "Sign me up!"

From what I gathered, it was going to be one heck of a trip. Seventeen days in total, beginning and ending with a 20-hour flight over an 8,000-mile stretch of ocean, across 15 time zones and the International Date Line and a wide scale of climate changes. Most significant to me, it would mark my first time to travel back to the ancestral homeland I hadn't seen in over four decades.

On several occasions over the years, I had entertained the thought of such a venture but had invariably faltered when confronted with the logistics. After all, Việt-Nam, having just opened its door in the last 25 years, is still a relatively new tourist destination in the midst of modernizing its infrastructures. But even more daunting than the challenge of mapping out a detailed itinerary, complete with hotel and transport accommodations, was a pervasive sense of uncertainty: Has the country healed from decades of brutal warfare, enough to welcome visitors with open arms? What is it like nowadays inside one of the last remaining communist regimes in the world? Would I find myself a lost stranger in the land of my childhood, thus confirming the perennial adage that one can never go home again?

But then when I learned that the tour in question was organized by an international travel company of good repute and that it would be headed by an experienced Vietnamese guide who would handle all the planning minutiae, I realized on the spot I had no more excuses. It was now or never: Time to discover the answers to my questions.

In the weeks that followed, I applied for the required entry visa through a service agency specializing in those matters, obtained the recommended inoculations, and began packing plenty of light clothing, sunscreen lotion, and rain protection gear. Then on a Friday night in late October 2016, in a fog of nervous excitement, I boarded a Boeing Triple Seven in LAX bound for Southeast Asia—my first trip home since I had left as a teenager.

This travelogue retraces the major segment of the tour—the final ten days—which took us through the length of Việt-Nam, from Sài-Gòn in the south to Hà-Nội in the north, stopping along the way in the central coastal cities of Hội-An and Huế and at Hạ-Long Bay on the Gulf of Tonkin. I have tried not only to recapture the highlights of this whirlwind journey—with their historical background and mythical lore—but also to explore a few special sites that I wish we could have squeezed into our packed schedule. At times the travelogue may read like a journal because it is sprinkled throughout with all kinds of resurrected memories—from my own childhood, in a time and place long since gone.

The book contains many pictures, 43 at last count. Most were taken by me on this trip—so please kindly overlook any imperfections—and the rest is generously contributed by family and friends who have visited there before. Color printing technology being where it is today, I have been forced to limit the total number of pictures and pages to reduce the setup and printing fees. This is so the book can be reasonably priced for a wide audience, even though my personal inclination is to share every relevant and worthwhile photograph I have.

On another note, I hope the reader will tolerate my decision to include many historic names in Vietnamese, along with their English translations, of course. As it was in our age-old tradition, names were never merely names; they carried great meaning and were often used to promulgate noble aspirations. Over the millennia, many of these ancient names also took on an extra aura as they became associated with momentous events that still resonate with the Vietnamese people to this day. By incorporating them into the travelogue in their original spellings, I strive to convey an intangible aspect of our heritage, one that extends beyond pictures and descriptive words.

To people who have read my book *Once upon a Mulberry Field* (Willow Stream Publishing, 2014), this travelogue offers a glimpse of the story's setting as it appears half a century later. For others, I hope it kindles your passion for travel and discovery and also provides you with a different view of this once ravaged land—and perhaps the inspiration to visit there some day. I now leave you with these enticing words from the French writer Marcel Proust: "The real voyage of discovery consists not in seeking new landscapes, but in having new eyes."

This journey across the Pacific Ocean accomplished both for me.

C. L. Hoàng
San Diego, October 2017

Chapter One

Rain, Sweet Rain

Friday, November 4

As the Airbus A321 shudders to a full stop, I close my eyes momentarily, take a deep breath, and exhale through my mouth.

We have just landed at Tân-Sơn-Nhất International Airport in Sài-Gòn, Việt-Nam.

After a few minutes' delay, the line of standing passengers begins to move. I clamber out of my seat, reach for my carry-on in the overhead bin, and follow the crowd off the plane. A shuttle bus takes us to the arrival terminal, where we file through the glass door and along the cordoned walkways to the immigration counters. Despite the sizable throng of foreign visitors, the paper processing goes smoothly. The unsmiling immigration officer checks my name and picture on the passport, looks up, and grumbles a few questions in Vietnamese. He makes a detailed note of my answers, then without a word hands me back my papers and waves me through.

In a daze, I wander out to the sprawling baggage claim area.

I'm back. Back on the soil where I grew up, for the first time in 40-plus years.

The mere notion makes my head spin. I feel an urge to jump and scream, but instead my feet just drag to a halt as my weary eyes dart around, trying in vain to latch onto something familiar. Only now does it strike me how huge and modern this place actually is. It's nothing like the cramped and noisy airport where my family came to see me off all those years ago. As memories flash back in bits and pieces, I hurry to collect my luggage and rejoin the rest of my tour group. Trí is our Vietnamese guide, a young-looking man born after the war, of slight build and friendly demeanor, with a clear accent. He encourages us with a smile, brandishes his long stick with the tour sign in lieu of a flag, and leads us out to the curbside where a full-sized coach is waiting.

It's dark by now, and the evening air feels humid but pleasantly balmy. It's such a welcome relief after the scorching heat and extreme mugginess in Bangkok, Thailand, and Siem Reap, Cambodia, where we had spent the first five days of the tour. As the big bus lumbers out onto the street that will take us into the center of Sài-Gòn, four miles away, I peer through the glass window at the surroundings. During the war, apart from the civilian airport, Tân-Sơn-Nhất also housed a USAF base, the second largest in South Việt-Nam after Biên-Hòa, as well as MACV Headquarters (the U.S. Military Assistance Command in the country) and the 3rd Field Hospital. There's no evidence any of those survived from that time. Instead, the street is now lined with imposing business and office buildings and lit up with neon signs and giant billboards. To the overcrowded ethnic quarters in Bangkok and the struggling countryside of Cambodia, the memories of which are still vivid in our minds, this flourishing face put on by Sài-Gòn offers an unexpected contrast that is almost breathtaking.

"Welcome to Hồ-Chí-Minh City or Sài-Gòn, the largest city in Việt-Nam, with a population of twelve million. . . . Yeah . . . the name Sài-Gòn is perfectly acceptable and still widely used."

Half-listening to Trí's voice over the bus speaker, my nose pressed up against the window, I gaze at the urban landscape scrolling by. Less than half an hour into the ride, we approach the city center and the road narrows even as the buildings on both sides grow taller and fancier. Our big coach gets snarled up in billowing, honking motor-scooter traffic that swarms and surges around it like giant schools of fish. At least *that* hasn't changed since the war years; if anything, it may have become worse. Through the glare of city lights, I strain my eyes to search for some familiar landmarks but find none.

Trí's voice snaps me out of my thoughts. "As far as exchange rates go, the higher your bills' denominations and the fresher and newer they look, the more favorable rates you're going to get. . . .Yeah . . . I can't explain to you why that is. It's just the way people here prefer their foreign currency. So whenever my wife gets upset at me for something and doesn't talk to me, I just go take out all my dollar bills and spend hours ironing them to make them look like new."

Amid the laughter, our tour bus turns onto a small street and slowly rolls halfway up the sidewalk to stop in front of a brightly lit hotel. It's a steel-and-glass high rise, the middle one of three such structures squeezed in side by side on that short block, all of them hotels. Led by our tireless guide, we stumble out of the bus and straggle up the wide steps into the sparkling lobby where we check in. As anxious as I have been to set out exploring immediately, by the time my luggage is delivered to my room I am dead on my feet. And with its getting late already, I opt for a warm shower and the soft and cozy hotel bed.

The next morning, after a refreshing night's sleep, I go down to breakfast in the ground floor restaurant off the lobby. Breakfast is served hot, buffet style, with a variety of both western and traditional Vietnamese selections. It is sheer delight for me to be able to enjoy *phở*, a tasty beef noodle soup, and *bánh cuốn*, steamed rice rolls, at such early hours in the morning, just like we used to do at home when I was a kid, eons ago. Besides making my stomach happy, the hotel has also impressed me with its well-appointed room and courteous service, proving that its four-star rating, as promised by the tour company, is no hype. But it isn't until I examine the downtown map over a cup of fragrant coffee that I come to appreciate the hotel's finest asset: its location.

Situated a mere few blocks off the very heart of downtown, our hotel looks like a leisurely 15- to 20-minute walk to where all the action and historic landmarks are. Since we have the morning free, I rush back to my room to grab my camera and an umbrella and then head out. The monsoon season is supposed to have wound down by this time of year, but a late front has blown in rainclouds that cover the sky and keep the temperature pleasant in spite of the stickiness.

Down the hotel steps, with map in hand, I take a moment to get my bearings. This area, which is close to a large hospital and the French Cultural Institute, used to have a mix of old houses and charming villas with gardens and wrought-iron gates. All those have now vanished, supplanted by gleaming high rises and new constructions that appear crammed into their lots. It reinforces my decision that I will not venture back to our former neighborhood, having been told by relatives who had visited there that it had completely changed and was now unrecognizable.

Some of the streets still retain their old names, and I feel more confident following those to the city center. With every step carrying me closer, a sense of quaint familiarity starts to take hold and my heartbeat quickens. The walks on the smaller side streets are still as narrow and uneven as I recall, buckled by mature trees that tower above them. My gaze flies up to the lacy foliage reminiscent of the jacaranda or the royal poinciana trees, only denser, and a warm feeling fills my heart at the sight of these tamarind trees, a beloved presence on the streets of Sài-Gòn since even before my time. Stepping around a motor-scooter parking lot that takes up most of the sidewalk, I turn the corner. And suddenly there it is, stretching ahead of me for many blocks down to the Sài-Gòn River—the most famous street in former French Indochina: Đồng-Khởi, or Tự-Do Street before 1975, also known as Rue Catinat under the French.

The street opens wide, and luxuriant trees along its spacious sidewalks form an inviting promenade lined with boutiques and restaurants. The buildings look new and attractive, with an architecture that evokes old-world charm in keeping with the French Colonial structures still dotting this district. Halfway down the block, something pops into my field of vision from across the street, stopping me in my tracks. With a quick inhale, I recognize the *grande dame* of Sài-Gòn's hôtellerie, the Hotel Continental.

The Hotel Continental (aka "the Continental Shelf" during the war).

Established in 1880, the four-story Continental was the first hotel built in Việt-Nam by the French. For more than a hundred years since, it has hosted many notable guests and was mentioned in novels by W. Somerset Maugham and Graham Greene—a long-term guest in room 214—and featured in the movies *The Quiet American* (first version, 1958) and *Indochine*. During the war, its open terrace-café on the ground floor served as a popular gathering place to foreign journalists, who nicknamed it "the (Continental) Shelf." *Newsweek* and *Time* magazines each had their wartime bureaus right above it, on the second floor. On a personal side note, the Shelf also provided the setting to an important scene in my book, *Once upon a Mulberry Field.*

The hotel had obviously gone through extensive refurbishment. While it has retained the essence of its original architecture and style, I am disappointed to find the historic Shelf now sedately enclosed behind windows, stripped of its open arches and awnings.

Meanwhile, Lam-Sơn Square, which stands adjacent to the Continental, is still kept free of traffic as in the old days to allow tourists to stroll up to the Opera House in the square center. "Built in 1898 in a flamboyant style of the [French] Third Republic" (W. Somerset Maugham), this distinctive-looking building boasts a half-dome façade decorated with stone-carved statues and ornaments. At one time, it was home to the National Assembly of South Việt-Nam. On the other side of the Opera House, directly facing the Continental, is the original Caravelle Hotel. When it opened its doors in 1959, this 10-story art-deco hotel was the tallest building in the city. It soon became a central headquarters for diplomats and journalists, housing the embassies of Australia and New Zealand, as well as the Sài-Gòn bureaus of the *New York Times*, the *Washington Post*, ABC, and CBS. Its balconied rooftop bar gained fame as an unofficial "press club," frequented by such newsmen as Neil Sheehan, Peter Arnett, and Walter Cronkite.

My eyes are drawn to the 24-story tower adjoined to the original structure. A 1998 addition aimed at ensuring the hotel's prominent standing in the fast-growing metropolis, it now comprises the bulk of the updated property. Behind it, all the way down to the river, soars the new cityscape of ever taller high rises.

Opera House and Caravelle Hotel, viewed from "the Continental Shelf."

Past Lam-Sơn Square, I head down the older section of Tự-Do Street. Here the road narrows and traffic begins to bog down. Tamarind trees still shade the sidewalks, which once again are buckled and cluttered, but outdated relics from the 1950s and '60s still hold their grounds against encroaching steel-and-glass giants. *But for how much longer?* I wonder as I stop across from Brodard, a café-restaurant that was somewhat of an institution in old Sài-Gòn. For *Mulberry Field* readers, this is the place where Roger Connors took his Vietnamese lady friend, Liên, or Lee Anne, on their first date. The big red sign overhanging the entrance to the now-closed building still proudly proclaims, "Brodard Bakery since 1948."

Continuing my walk, I amble past the historic Grand Hotel (former Saigon Palace, ca. 1930), whose façade with its picturesque cupola is overshadowed by a recent addition, a 20-story luxury wing. A block down from the Grand, overlooking the wharf and the river, sits the regal Majestic Hotel in the classic French Riviera style, a major landmark of Sài-Gòn since 1925. Graham Greene's protagonist in *The Quiet American*, Tom Fowler, had put the hotel's rooftop bar on the literary map when he lamented, withered from the day's heat, "You couldn't believe it would ever be seven o'clock and cocktail time on the roof of the Majestic, with a wind from Saigon River." Fowler, however, would have winced at the torrential traffic now churning on the streets below, at the corners where old Tự-Do terminates into a thoroughfare that stretches along the river. I stare longingly across the busy avenue at the Bạch-Đằng Wharf. Our parents used to take us kids there in the evenings so we could catch a breeze and run and play. But another look at the sea of motorcycles sweeping by—sometimes with an entire family of four riding on the same bike, the little children clinging to their parents—and I know I don't dare cross. So I mosey past the arched façade of the Majestic, round the next corner onto Nguyễn-Huệ Street, which runs parallel to Tự-Do, and head back the other way.

Flower market on Nguyễn-Huệ Street before Tết.

The view opens up before me, the preexisting median island having been broadened into a spectacular pedestrian way. Every year around Tết—our traditional Vietnamese New Year—a beautiful flower market would assemble on the island, signaling us kids we were soon to receive red envelopes of *li-xì* (lucky money) from the adults.

Now, with this expanded walkway, I have heard the market has become a true annual extravaganza, eagerly awaited by locals and tourists alike. On either side of the street, shimmering towers rise in clashing contrast to the humble and much rundown buildings from the war days, a testament to the continual change undergone by the city. A singular symbol of the new time is the 68-story Bitexco Financial Tower. Boasting a non-rooftop helipad that juts out from its 52nd floor, it is currently the tallest edifice in Sài-Gòn, and its slim profile can be seen from any vantage point around downtown.

Reflection of the 68-story Bitexco Financial Tower.

It starts to sprinkle, so I rush down the pedestrian way toward another historic landmark in the city center: the Rex Hotel. During the war, American generals used to stay at this five-story refurbished trade center, earning it the nickname "the Generals' Hotel." It also housed the Joint U.S. Public Affairs Office, or JUSPAO, which conducted daily briefings on the war, dubbed the "Five O'Clock Follies" by skeptical reporters. With a clear view of the river, the Officers' Club on the rooftop—now an al-fresco restaurant-bar sought out by history buffs—was a well-known hangout for military officials and their journalist guests. These days, the Rex, like most other luxury hotels in the country, is state-owned and operated.

Rex Hotel (aka "the Generals' Hotel" during the war).

Although extensively renovated, the Rex has retained its original 1950s style, down to the crown logo that surmounts its façade. But huge building projects are underway all around it that are further changing the face of the city. The nearby iconic Tax Shopping Center, after 136 years of continuous service, was torn down recently to await the erection of a 40-story replacement. Just steps away from the Rex entrance, construction has commenced on the underground metro line that will service downtown and connect it to an amusement park on the outskirts. Out of habit from childhood, my eyes still search for the old *bùng binh* (traffic circle) and decorative fountain at the intersection of Nguyễn-Huệ and Lê-Lợi Streets, now long since removed to make way for the pedestrian walk.

Turning away from the hotel, I arrive in front of the centerpiece at the end of the pedestrian way: the former City Hall (Toà Đô-Chánh), fronted by a beautifully landscaped square. Modeled after the Hôtel de Ville of Paris but on a smaller scale, it was completed in 1908. Its red-tile roofs and ornate yellow-and-cream-colored façade most often described as "gingerbread" have made it a popular tourist attraction and probably the most photographed building in the city.

Old City Hall.

Between the square in front of the City Hall and the Hotel Continental on old Tự-Do Street, there used to stand an indoor mall and office-apartment complex known as Passage Eden. In the war years, many journalists and broadcasters lived and worked there as both the Associated Press and NBC News maintained their offices on the building's fourth floor. In *Once upon a Mulberry Field*, the reporter Dick Hayashi also kept an apartment there where events took place that would profoundly change the lives of the main protagonists.

In 2010 Passage Eden was demolished, and with it went the cinema theater of the same name, the ice cream parlor Givral (mentioned in *The Quiet American*), and the bookstore Xuân Thu—all part of my childhood paradise. Today, rising in its footprint is an elegant contemporary building, four stories high. With a modern pastel color theme and glittery windows, the Union Square Shopping Mall is the newest high-end retail center in Sài-Gòn and home to many flagship stores of top luxury brands.

Inside Vincom Shopping Center.

We are supposed to meet at the hotel for an afternoon guided tour, so I begin to head back. Kitty-corner from the Union Square Mall, on Tự-Do Street, are the striking blue-glass towers of Vincom Center, where I've been told more upscale shops and restaurants can be found. Since the morning sprinkle has turned into larger drops, I decide to duck out of the rain by cutting through the main level of these twin towers, which are on my way. Inside the mall, the largest in the city, a central bank of escalators links the 200-plus shops that occupy the lower seven floors. Crowds stroll leisurely around, happy to look, shop, and eat. I feel my head spinning. All this luxury and money—where has it all come from? Foreign investment? Tourist dollars? Isn't this the same capitalistic lifestyle that had sparked the ideological war in the past, pitting North against South for a deadly quarter-century—now embraced with unbridled enthusiasm?

Taking a side street from the mall exit, I stumble on a throwback scene from earlier days: a woman street vendor sitting on a low stool on the sidewalk, her shoulder pole and two baskets of steamy foods on the ground next to her. Toy-sized plastic trays and chairs are arranged around her into a makeshift diner. This way, she can pick up everything and take off at a moment's notice, in case the police show up. Meanwhile, her business seems to be thriving with workers on lunch break from nearby shops and offices. A microcosm of survival economy, poking through the glossy veneer of prosperity, here in the city center. What is life like out in the countryside?

I return to the hotel just as my tour group is gathering around our guide, Trí, in the lobby.

"We're going to walk first," he says. "Bring an umbrella, and don't forget your headsets."

In the drizzle, we retrace some of my morning route before Trí leads us down the other end of old Tự-Do Street, away from the river and downtown. As we troop past the Vincom Center, he points through the dripping foliage of tamarind trees at a craggy old building on the next street over. "That is where the famous helicopter evacuation took place in April 1975," he says, "the one captured in the photograph everyone thought was of the American Embassy."

With a chill, I recognize the dilapidated structure—the old CIA Building in Sài-Gòn, also known as the Pittman Apartments, at 22 Gia-Long Street (now Lý-Tự-Trọng). Instantly my mind races back to that final day of the war, filling in the rest of the picture: the chopper precariously perched across the elevator engine room on the rooftop, with a crewman leaning out to help a line of desperate refugees scrambling up a steep ladder—the very scene dramatized in the climax of the stage musical *Miss Saigon*. Straggling behind the group, my hair and face wet with rain, I snap my own photograph of the historic setting.

Old CIA Building (Pittman Apartments) in Sài-Gòn.

The next stop is the Notre-Dame Cathedral Basilica of Sài-Gòn, standing in a wide open square a block away from the former Pittman Apartments. Constructed by the French between 1863 and 1880 in neo-Romanesque style, with the two bell towers added on later in 1895, this largest church in Việt-Nam has always been a beloved sight, especially popular at Christmastime no matter what your faith. I remember as a kid coming down here on Christmas Eves with my siblings and cousins, so thrilled to mingle among the outdoor throngs of celebrators. Another childhood memory pops into my head—of a cozy bookstore around here, whose name I can't recall, that my friends and I used to hike to after school to peek at its stash of French comic books. Earnestly scanning, I can find no trace left of our favorite reading nook.

Notre-Dame Cathedral Basilica of Sài-Gòn.

Following closely behind Trí, we cross the busy street along the cathedral square and reach an imposing ochre-colored building covered with arched windows and green shutters—the Sài-Gòn Central Post Office. Touted as the grandest post office in Southeast Asia, this neo-classical structure took four years to build (1886–1891). It was the final and crowning achievement of French architect Marie-Alfred Foulhoux, whose many buildings still grace the capital's urban landscape. On either side of the entrance hangs a huge wall map, one of old Sài-Gòn and the other of the early telegraph network between South Việt-Nam and Cambodia. The cavernous interior resembles a late 19th-century European railroad station with its soaring vaulted ceiling and glass canopy supported by graceful columns, its high windows along the walls, and a beautiful patterned tiled floor. Everything in here—from the numerous wickets and alcoves to the ornate colonial furnishings and original phone booths—speaks of a bygone time and place. As a child, I sometimes came with my dad and later rode my bicycle here to buy stamps and mail letters, but I don't think I ever fully appreciated how magnificent and special this building was.

Central Post Office of Sài-Gòn.

Outside the Post Office, along the curb, our tour bus is waiting to take the group to our next stop, a lacquerware factory a little way from the city center. It is more of a gallery with a small workshop in front where we can watch the artisans plying their craft. I've always enjoyed these traditional artworks but this is my first time to witness at close range the painstaking, labor-intensive process whereby the base wood is polished, then painted or inlaid with fine bits of duck eggshell or mother-of-pearl, and finally varnished with a wide palette of colored lacquers. The exquisite finished products, astounding in their richness and beauty, are displayed in full view in the grand showroom where we wander about endlessly, gawking and admiring. The high price tags are obviously geared toward foreign visitors, but any souvenir hunters worth their salt may still find a few reasonable bargains to take home with them.

After giving everyone enough time to browse and shop, Trí gathers us up and shepherds us back to the bus for our final destination of the afternoon.

"Sorry we have to rush a little bit," he says. "It is getting late and I really want you to see our next stop in daylight, at its busiest and most fun. We are now taking a short ride to Chợ Bến-Thành, the city's Central Market at the opposite end of downtown. The driver will drop us off, and we will take a walking tour all around it. It's a big place."

The mere mention of the name brings back to me a world of colors, sounds, and smells, of frantic motion and excitement—the beating heart of Sài-Gòn's everyday life, now as then. Built in 1912 at a major intersection downtown, Chợ Bến-Thành remains one of the city's best-known landmarks and features a prominent clock tower that dominates the neighborhood. Its red-tile roof provides shelter to hundreds of vending booths piled high with anything that is commonly eaten, worn, or used by the locals, or with souvenir items that appeal to tourists. Dining stalls are scattered throughout the market that serve hawker-style Vietnamese cuisine and cold drinks to the hungry and thirsty. As tempting as it all smells and looks, I'm reminded of Trí's cautionary tales about street food and decide to pass on it. Ever so helpful, he also gives us shopping tips. "Feel free to bargain," says our guide, with a nod. "Yeah . . . it's kind of how business is done here." My most vivid memory of Chợ Bến-Thành is of its festive atmosphere before Tết, the lunar-calendar New Year, when the market was packed to its rafters with holiday trappings: traditional prepared foods wrapped in banana leaf, fruit and candies, potted flowers, firecrackers, joss sticks, candles—a delightful, mesmerizing spectacle to kids of all ages.

Exiting this hub of frenzied activity, we go wait by the bus for the group's stragglers. Trí points to a restaurant on the second floor of a tired building across the street. It appears just another nondescript eatery, except for the flashy sign that screams "Phở 2000."

"That's the noodle place where President Clinton and his daughter Chelsea ate during their visit to Sài-Gòn in 2000." Trí chuckles. "It has since become a tourist attraction."

The rain, which has stopped for some time, starts sprinkling again so we all clamber onto the big coach. I've planned to walk back to the hotel along the wide Lê-Lợi Street to view more of downtown and to check whether the popular Nước Mía Viễn Đông is still around. For *Mulberry Field* readers, this is the sugar-cane juice stand where Liên took Roger when she was giving him the city tour. But with the pavement now glistening wet, I'm just happy to ride back with the group. There are at least two other special places I wish I'd had time to visit: my former high school, and especially the Sài-Gòn Zoo and Botanical Garden, both mere strolls away, though in opposite directions, from Notre-Dame Cathedral.

The zoo, which is said to be the eighth oldest in the world, and its botanical garden have always been among the city's most beloved treasures. Founded in 1865 by the French after they conquered Sài-Gòn, it's a green oasis of exotic plants and animals, a sprawling refuge from the heat and the hustle and bustle of the capital. Also located within its grounds are the Museum of Vietnamese History, whose architecture was inspired by the Summer Palace in Beijing, and the Temple of Remembrance, built in the same traditional style as the imperial mausoleums in Huế and dedicated to the 18 Kings Hùng, the nation's founding ancestors. Both monuments were added in the 1920s. The park has always proved a popular attraction, not only to children—some of my fondest times and memories as a kid took place there—but to adults as well, especially young couples, because of its romantic setting. In fact, *Mulberry Field* readers may remember that it was at a lotus pond in the park, in the shade of centuries-old royal poinciana trees, where Roger first fell in love with Liên.

But since we're leaving in the morning, both the zoo and botanical garden and my former high school will have to wait until another time. Twenty-four hours are simply not enough to get a feel for even a concentrated area like downtown Sài-Gòn, let alone the whole city. Personally, I could spend a few weeks here, if not longer, just wandering the streets and retracing footsteps from days gone by. For that alone, I hope to return one day soon for a more leisurely visit.

Back at the hotel, after a quick shower and rest, I head down to old Tự-Do Street to exchange for more *đồng*, the local money, and to get some dinner. It's our second and last evening in Sài-Gòn. Luckily, the drizzle has let up again and a gentle breeze from the river is rustling the tamarind trees and cooling the air. The exchange counter happens to be across a side street from Brodard, the closed bakery and café, and diagonally from it is a noodle shop that caught my eye earlier in the day. I decide to give it a try. The food tastes good, and the waiter is a pleasant young man with a ready smile. Working here part-time while enrolled at a two-year college, he's a beneficiary of the booming tourist industry who seems very appreciative of his opportunity. As I get ready to leave, the rain returns, this time with a vengeance. There's no chance I can walk back without getting drenched, even with an umbrella and only a few blocks to go. So the helpful young man flags down a taxi for me; then sloshing through the downpour and flooded streets, it drops me right to the front steps of the hotel.

The hard rain continues unabated through the rest of the evening. By the time I turn out the lights and crawl under the covers, I can still hear it tapping against the window—the comforting lullaby of my youth. Slowly sinking in like the heaviness on my eyelids is the warm realization that I'm truly here, back in the city where I once was a child. So much has changed. How could it not have? But I'm thankful there are still enough remnants from that time to help me navigate my way around. The old buckled sidewalks still retain echoes of the past, and the surviving landmarks have seemed like long lost friends. But there is no feeling like the way I felt strolling under the tamarind trees once again, even in the afternoon shower. As images tumble around in my head, mixing past with present, sleep overcomes me.

The next morning, I get up early to pack before heading downstairs to the hotel buffet. Overnight the storm has cleared out, and a hazy sun is breaking through. After breakfast, as I'm leaving the restaurant, I hear commotion in the lobby. A woman on my tour rushes up from behind and whispers excitedly, "There's a big wedding just underway." It turns out to be not just any wedding, but a traditional one. Two rows of smiling bridesmaids and groomsmen line the steps outside the hotel entrance, the women dressed in yellow-silk and the men in red-brocade traditional garbs, which consist of a long gown called *áo dài*, with matching headdress. In their arms they carry round trays wrapped in red cloth. According to custom, these contain offerings that will be presented on the ancestral altar, which has probably been set up in a ceremonial hall inside. A big tray holding a roasted piglet is carefully handled by the head groomsman, who is now leading the procession into the hotel. What a treat—and an auspicious sign, if popular lore is to be trusted—to witness this happy event on our last morning in Sài-Gòn. Hotel guests gather around and snap photos as the wedding party pile into the elevators.

By ten o'clock our group has checked out of the hotel and is on the bus to the airport. We're flying out to Đà-Nẵng on the Central Coast for our second leg of the tour. Through the window I survey the street scene in daylight, searching again for any vestiges from the past—

quaint villas behind closed gates interspersed with clumps of tin-roofed shanties, as used to be seen along this road to Tân-Sơn-Nhất. We drive by an important-looking Buddhist temple, the largest in the city according to Trí: Vĩnh-Nghiêm (Ever Solemn) Pagoda, whose eight-story tower soars above its surroundings. But apart from that, I see nothing but side-by-side storefronts and office buildings. The traffic reflects this urban growth, looking as gnarly as in downtown. By now, however, I'm no longer shocked by it, my senses having adapted to the frenetic pulse of the city. And just as my heart is starting to sync up to this familiar beat, it's already time to leave.

One last look at Sài-Gòn traffic.

The bus pulls up in front of the terminal and I notice it's a different building than the one we arrived in, less than 48 hours ago; more modest in size, and older looking.

"This is the domestic terminal," Trí clarifies. "The original airport. The other night we were at the new international terminal, which has only been in operation since 2007."

It makes sense that Tân-Sơn-Nhất, ranked among the top 50 busiest airports in the world in 2015, needs more than one terminal to handle its high traffic volume, which is said to be upwards of 20 million passengers per year and growing. It also explains my confusion two days ago when, after landing, I did not recognize anything familiar. But now we are at the original airport, where my family and relatives came to say goodbye a lifetime ago, when I left to go to college in America. As I drag my luggage inside the terminal and head for the check-in counter, memories of that unforgettable day lurk around every corner. The terminal has clearly been renovated from floor to ceiling and bears little resemblance to its former self, but my throat still catches, just knowing that this was the farewell place all those years ago.

We wait an hour before boarding. As the airplane taxies onto the runway, I catch a blurred reflection in the window—of a scrawny kid fresh out of high school, leaving home and his family for the first time, squinting back at the receding terminal. Never could he have imagined that it would take 40 years before he was able to return.

Hopefully, now he won't have to wait another 40 years for his next trip home.

Chapter Two

The Old Streets of Faifo

Sunday, November 6

Throughout the war, traveling was restricted due to safety and security concerns. That's why I'm so looking forward to this phase of our tour, which will take us to parts of the country I have never visited before. It begins here in Đà-Nẵng, where we arrive in late morning.

With a population of over a million, Đà-Nẵng is the third largest city in Việt-Nam and home to the country's third international airport (after Sài-Gòn and Hà-Nội). Its location on the estuary of the Hàn River has made it a major port on the Central Coast since the mid-19th century, and its airport used to be one of the busiest in the world in the 1960s and early '70s, when it was hosting a large U.S. air base. The city has always held a special place in my heart as my birthplace, even though my family did not stay here very long. As we step off the plane and file into the terminal, I keep telling myself, almost in awe and disbelief, that it wasn't far from here, in a nearby hospital that may still be standing, that I came into this world decades ago.

The terminal looks modern and spacious but not overwhelming, about the same size as Tân-Sơn-Nhất's domestic terminal where we took off. According to our Vietnamese guide, Trí, it was renovated from top to bottom and then reopened as a brand new terminal in 2011. For some reason our bus is not permitted to pull up to the curb out front, so after collecting our luggage we follow Trí a short distance to the parking lot where the large coach awaits.

"Downtown is just a mile and a half north of the airport," Trí announces. "But we are going south to Hội-An, which is twenty miles, or a half-hour drive, from here."

The good auspices of this morning's wedding must be rubbing off on us since the day turns out gorgeous: humid but bright and sunny, with billowy white clouds against a porcelain-blue backdrop. The Central Coast has a climate different from the South's, being mostly affected by the northeast monsoon that has only now begun to bring heavy showers. The bus exits the airport and turns onto a highway that parallels the coastline. Gazing across the road, I watch a white sandy beach flit by, hemmed in by walkways and palm trees on one side and aqua-blue water on the other and stretching as far south as the eye can see.

"Welcome to Mỹ-Khê Beach, also known to American soldiers as China Beach," Trí says. "Yeah . . . it's among the most beautiful beaches in Việt-Nam."

China Beach (between Đà-Nẵng and Hội-An).

During the war, this was home to the 510th Evacuation Hospital and the popular "Five and Dime" R&R center, made famous by a TV series in the early '80s. The beach owes its nickname to its sparkling china-white sand. That, along with excellent surf, has earned it a recent spot on *Forbes Magazine's* list of the "World's Most Luxurious Beaches."

This in turn has attracted the biggest names in the international hotel and resort industry, which rush in to erect hotel high rises and five-star resorts with casinos and golf courses all along the pristine coast. Unfortunately, we are told, this frenzied development has been carried out without adequate planning or regulation, so the beach access is often blocked to the local public.

"Doesn't it look just like South Florida?" asks the woman in the seat ahead of me as she turns to her companion, who nods in agreement.

About 15 minutes into our trip, Trí calls our attention to a cluster of hills rising abruptly from the narrow plain inland. "You see that limestone and marble rock group over there?" he says. "It's called Ngũ-Hành-Sơn. Five mountains, named after the five classic elements: Metal, Wood, Water, Fire, and Earth. U.S. soldiers used to know them as Marble Mountains."

Back in the war years there used to be a helicopter facility at the base of those big hills, the Marble Mountain Air Facility, operated primarily by the U.S. Marine Corps and later by the U.S. Army, then the South Vietnamese Air Force. Trí squints out the window. "You cannot see them from here, but there are pagodas up on top of the mountains. They've got good view all around, so Communist soldiers used to hide in them to spy on the Americans down below."

I turn away from the hills. Even decades after the war has ended, we are still surrounded with vestiges and reminders of it everywhere we go. Memories and emotions still run strong, vivid and ready to spring to life at the slightest evocation. It all seems so neat now, so peaceful and idyllic, but I remember well a time when it wasn't like this—quite the opposite, in fact.

As if reading my thoughts, Trí promptly moves on. "Okay. Let me tell you a little about the place we're headed to, Hội-An. Its name means 'peaceful meeting place.' Between the 15th and 19th centuries, it was a thriving seaport called Hải-Phố, which means 'seaside town.'

European traders mispronounced it as Faifo and referred to the place by that name." He pauses to recollect his facts before continuing, "Today it's no longer a seaport. Yeah . . . only a small town of one hundred and twenty thousand people. But its historic district has been well preserved and was declared a UNESCO World Heritage Site in 1999."

The bus slows down as it enters the town on a narrow street bordered by trees and quaint-looking houses painted in yellow and adorned with balconies and shutters. A definite old French influence, from the colonial days. It's early afternoon in the small town so the traffic seems light, even with motor scooters screaming by. Our full-sized coach pulls over to a complete stop.

"The historic district is a pedestrian zone, so we have to park out here and walk in," says Trí. "But just wait here by the bus while I go buy the tickets."

He soon returns with tickets in hand, pulls his mike out from his pocket, and turns it on. "Put on your headsets, please. We will now enter Old Town through the Chinese quarter." Waving his guide's stick with the tour sign attached to the tip in lieu of a flag, he leads the way and our troop falls in behind him. The temperature has been steadily rising, making it very hot and sticky now.

In its heyday, Hội-An, or Hải-Phố (Faifo), became the most important seaport on the South China Sea, thanks to its central location on the emerging spice trade route. It attracted merchants from all over, including the Chinese, Japanese, Indians, Dutch, and Portuguese, and later the French and the English. But only two of those groups—the Chinese and the Japanese—settled permanently in their own quarters and left their distinct imprints on the town. By the early 19th century, Hội-An began to see its eminent status quickly eroded by a new rival port just to the north, Đà-Nẵng. Local historians claim this was because the Thu-Bồn River, on whose estuary the town sat, was silting up.

The decline continued unabated over the next two centuries as Hội-An further receded into obscurity, concealing all its architectural treasures in a kind of time capsule that has been miraculously spared even through the war years.

We follow Trí onto a street swamped with foot traffic that recalls the vacationing mobs on the medieval streets of Europe. You bump into people wherever you turn, making it impossible to take any pictures without some tourist drifting unaware into your viewfinder. Lining the street are narrow houses, most of them single-story and sheltered by mossy tile roofs that sag under the weight of centuries. They are the so-called "tube houses" because they run deep in length to make up for their restricted width. Traditionally the front room would function as a shop, separated by a courtyard from the living quarters in the back. In the 2002 screen adaptation of Graham Greene's *The Quiet American*, many street scenes of old Sài-Gòn in the 1950s were actually filmed in this neighborhood. Meandering through one such shop-house, we travel back in time as we admire its sculpted beams and columns, its ancestral chapel and recessed stairway to a hidden loft, and its fabulous antique furniture.

A little way down the block, Trí stops in front of what looks like an ornate temple gate. "This is the Phúc-Kiến Assembly Hall, the grandest example of the type of community halls built by Chinese merchants who settled in Hội-An," he says. "Let's go in and have a look around, and while we're here I will pay so we can use their restroom facilities."

Phúc-Kiến is the Vietnamese-sounding name for Fukien, or Fujian, a Chinese province. Many of the merchants who migrated here had fled from their native provinces in China after the downfall of the Ming Dynasty in 1644. We cross a tiled courtyard decorated with bonsai plants in ceramic pots to enter the sprawling complex, which was founded in 1690. Besides serving as the meeting place for the

Phúc-Kiến natives, it also houses a temple to Thiên-Hậu, Goddess of the Sea, who is regarded as the protector of sailors. Her statue presides over the main altar in the elaborate front hall, flanked by her two assistants: the goddess Thuận-Phong-Nhĩ, who is said to be able to hear the sound of a shipwreck from a thousand miles away; and Thiên-Lý-Nhãn, the goddess who can see that distant ship in distress. To the right of the altar is a detailed model of the sailing junk that was used in the initial sea crossing from Phúc-Kiến to Việt-Nam. Various symbolic and mythical animals—fish, turtle, unicorn, dragon, phoenix—are prominently featured in sculptures and fountains scattered throughout the temple.

Phúc-Kiến Assembly Hall in Hội-An.

Hearing commotion in the courtyard, I round back to the front to witness the women in my tour group clinging to each other, bent over with laughter. They're all gathered outside the women's facility, its door flung open, with Trí standing to the side holding a roll of toilet paper for anyone who may need it, as he always does at every rest stop. The woman next to me tries to explain between nervous chortles. "Valerie, she was in there taking care of business while the rest of us waited out here, when all of a sudden we heard a loud shriek. Then she came barging out, white as a sheet. She . . . she . . ." The woman shudders and makes a face. "This nasty cockroach had landed right on her shoulder! Long whiskers it had, too. . . . We all just flipped out. Thank goodness someone grabbed her and flicked the darned thing off of her."

After the excitement subsides, we leave the assembly hall and continue down the street. It feels like a sweltering summer fair as we rejoin the throngs of visitors and saunter past shops, restaurants, and outdoor cafés along the roadsides. Also vying for a piece of the business are women street vendors who carry, bowing under the weight, their precious load of homemade food in baskets that swing from their shoulder pole. Even though Trí has warned us about street food, a couple of women from our group still stop to buy from these vendors. "Just to help them out a little," they say with a kind smile.

At the end of the street, we arrive before a narrow gate-like entrance with a tile roof over it. "We are now at the best-known landmark of Hội-An, considered by many its emblem," says Trí. "The Japanese Covered Bridge, also called Chùa Cầu, which means 'Bridge Pagoda.' You cross the bridge from this entrance in order to reach the old Japanese quarter on the other side."

Japanese Covered Bridge in Hội-An at sunset.

This graceful short bridge over a small tributary of the Thu-Bồn River was built around 1623 by the Japanese trading community, which had settled on the west side of the town, to link it with the Chinese quarter to the east. A Vietnamese temple was added into the northern section of the structure in the early 18th century. Above the entrance hangs a wooden sign with three Chinese characters engraved on it. Trí catches me staring at it and says, "That's the official name of the bridge up there on the sign. Yeah . . . it is said that the lord Nguyễn-Phúc-Chu passed by this way in 1719 and he named the bridge Lai-Viễn-Kiều, or 'bridge for friends from afar.'"

The sun is setting, so the group jostles to take photos before the last daylight fades, which seems to happen surprisingly fast. Before we're finished, the lights on the bridge have turned on, soon followed by color spotlights around the stone pillars, casting shimmering reflections on the dark water. Even with the sun down, it still feels warm and humid, but thankfully a cool breeze sweeps in from the river and brings some welcome relief.

Trí waves his guide's stick skyward. "Watch the lanterns overhead," he urges. "They're one of Hội-An's famous handicrafts, and they're about to light up anytime now."

As if on cue, strings of colorful lanterns that crisscross the street from one side to the other start flickering on to the audible delight of the crowd, soon illuminating the festive street scene and electrifying the already buoyant atmosphere. Delicious aromas of freshly cooked food waft out from cafés and restaurants where smiling hostesses wait by the door and beckon passersby to stop in. Trí leads our group to one of the nicer-looking places, most likely a good choice judging by the size of its clientele. He must have a reservation because the restaurant owner—a short, plump guy with a big voice and a ready laugh—personally greets us at the door and takes us to our private tables on the second floor. After a long, exciting day that has left all of us drained and famished, it's almost decadent pleasure to be able to sit down in an air-conditioned room and to be served the most delectable traditional Vietnamese dinner. Through the course of the meal, the owner, who speaks excellent English and has an endearing sense of humor, keeps regaling us with jokes, songs, and explanations about all the exotic food we're consuming.

After dinner, we have some time to wander around on our own, so I cross the open Hội-An footbridge to the other side of the river. On the esplanade by the water, a night market is bursting to life under even more splendid lanterns that shed light on all manner of vending stalls. It's such a lovely, fun scene that no less than three local newly-wed couples, with brides and grooms all decked out in traditional attire and accompanied by their happy entourage, have come out here to pose for their wedding pictures. Intrigued tourists surround the handsome couples to admire and cheer and snap photos. Some of the visitors are so fascinated by the tradition on display they even accost the newlyweds to have a souvenir picture taken with them, to which the couples, very gracious and understanding, oblige with a smile.

I pick up a few mementos from the street vendors and decide to practice my bargaining skills, as Trí suggested we always do. In the end, however, I'm happy to pay more than I probably should when I sense how much each sale means to the vendors and their families. Most of them are locals from the countryside hoping to sell a few trinkets to supplement their meager income. Then, my bag of treasures in hand, I head back across the footbridge to our rendezvous spot. After everyone has gathered, we follow Trí and exit the pedestrian zone to where the bus is waiting to pick us up. From there it takes us to our hotel, 15 minutes away from Old Town and about halfway to the popular Cửa Đại (or Big Gate) Beach.

Hội-An street scene at night.

As the bus pulls up in front of a six-story building set back from a small lush garden, Trí points to the other side of the street. "See the lady waving welcome to us on the sidewalk over there?" he asks. "She operates a laundry service, and she charges by weight rather than by the piece like at the hotel. If you like, you can drop off your dirty clothes tonight and she will have them washed and back to you by tomorrow evening." He raises a hand to quiet down the excited group—and no wonder, since after a week on the road we're all about to run out of fresh things to wear. "Wait, wait. There's more. Next to her place, on the right, is a custom tailor shop. They can make any clothes for you there: suit, shirt, gown, you name it. And they have lots of fabrics you can choose from. What they will do is take your measurements tonight and have your piece ready for you to try on in twenty-four hours. Hội-An is well-known for this type of services."

Off the bus, we cross the tropical garden and step inside a small but sparkling lobby, where we check in. As I'm finished getting processed and receive my card key, a light tug at my elbow makes me turn around. A young man dressed in simple hotel uniform beams at me.

"*Anh người Việt hả*—are you Vietnamese?" he asks. I have barely nodded before he goes on excitedly in our native tongue. "Welcome back! Is this your first time back visiting? My name is Tuấn. I'm so happy to meet you. I work here, and I will bring your luggage to your room."

As promised, Tuấn knocks on my door a short while later, hauls in my luggage, and sets it on the rack. Then he proceeds to show me how to operate all the controls, especially the one for the air conditioner. "I know you need to set it really cold so you can sleep," he says with a grin. "It must feel hot to you here, doesn't it?" Tuấn confides that he only works part time at the hotel while attending college and really loves his job. "It's an incredible opportunity for me. The pay is not bad, and I get to practice my English with foreign tourists. But what I enjoy the most is to meet Vietnamese people from overseas, like yourself. What's life like over in America? I always want to know." We chat some more, then he says goodnight to go finish his round of luggage delivery. What a heartwarming welcome, I'm still telling myself an hour later as I turn out the lights and slip into bed. For the first time on the trip, it really feels like I have come home.

The next morning, after a buffet-style breakfast in the hotel that features both Vietnamese and western choices, we depart for the pier, where a boat is waiting to take us on a cruise on the Thu-Bồn River. As we gingerly climb aboard the covered motorboat, an observant tour member comments on how unusually quiet the hotels along the riverbank appear.

"We're in the middle of the rainy season on the Central Coast," Trí explains. "The river is known to overflow, and when it does, these beautiful hotels here are in danger of being flooded. It's why most of them shut down during these months."

But once again, the weather gods have favored us with a rainless morning, highlighted by fluffy white clouds and a hazy sun. As soon as the boat launches, a refreshing breeze picks up and sweeps away the mugginess, and we know we're off to a pleasant excursion up the river. Comfortably settled in our seats, with the wind in our hair, we dreamily watch the countryside and islands drift by while listening to Trí share the tales of the region.

It so happens that centuries ago the Thu-Bồn River served as border between Việt-Nam and Champa (or Chàm), an ancient maritime kingdom that used to occupy most of the Central Coast until it was conquered by its neighbor to the north. Trà-Kiệu, the site of the Chàm former capital, lies twenty miles inland from Hội-An. Nothing is left of the ancient city except remnants of its rectangular ramparts. However, a complex of over 70 Hindu temples and tombs, built between the 4th and 14th centuries, still stands today in nearby Mỹ-Sơn Valley. In 1999, those ruins, some of which had survived the war in fairly good condition, were designated a World Heritage Site by UNESCO. In fact, a couple from our group has decided to forgo the boat cruise this morning so they can take an exploration trip to Mỹ-Sơn instead.

"Most of you in this tour group were just at Angkor Wat last week," Trí says. "Mỹ-Sơn is like a mini Angkor Wat, very similar in architecture but on a smaller scale."

I let my eyes roam over the bucolic scenery—sky, fields, river—trying to imagine it as the battleground where the Chàm and Vietnamese armies fought to the death to stake their claim on the land. Middle-school history lessons are coming back to me, most vividly the fascinating story of the Vietnamese princess Huyền-Trân. She was the daughter of King Trần Nhân Tôn, who in 1306 gave her in a political marriage to the king of Chàm. As part of the betrothal gifts from the royal groom to his bride, Champa ceded some territory north of Đà-Nẵng to Việt-Nam. But just a year later the king of Chàm passed away, and the country's tradition dictated that Huyền-Trân and all his other wives be cremated along with him. Upon hearing the news, the Vietnamese king dispatched a trusted young general to Champa under the guise of attending the royal funeral, but his real mission was to rescue the princess and bring her back by boat. The trip home took a year. As kids, we used to snicker and wonder out loud why it should have taken so long. It boggles my mind now, as I admire the serene landscape, to think that all that intrigue and history actually unfolded right around here.

"Get your cameras ready," Trí suddenly calls out, jolting me from my reverie. "Over there! As soon as we get closer, those fishermen will cast their net so you can take pictures."

Our motorboat slows down and approaches a small canoe with two fishermen on it, one of them manning the steering oar, the other standing with a droopy net in his hand. We all rush to the side of the boat nearest them, cameras and cell phones pointing. Trí yells out instructions to the men then begins his countdown. On his count of three, the fisherman throws his net up and out in one sweeping motion, forming a perfect circular web that floats down to the water like a parachute. Exclamations rise from all sides as camera shutters click away.

"He's using a special yellow net so we can see better," says Trí. "Now we will go around to the other side and he will cast the net one more time for us, from that angle."

To everyone's delight, we get to watch the man demonstrate his skill once again, allowing us another round of photos. Up close, his partner turns out to be a woman, maybe his wife. The two, middle-aged and wearing *nón lá*, the ubiquitous conical hat for shading against the sun, retrieve their net from the water then pull up alongside the boat to show us the catch within it. Trí pays them for their trouble, and we smile and wave goodbye to them as they row away.

"This is a good way for them to earn some extra income," Trí explains. "Now that they're done showing us, they will return to their day's real work. And we're also moving on, to our next stop at a village renowned for its handicraft carpentry."

Our boat picks up speed and winds its way through a labyrinth of sparsely populated islands. It sputters past a lone fisherman perched on his one-man skiff, his net and one bare leg dangling in the muddy water. From a distance, he looks small and almost blends into the sky and river—an immobile silhouette biding time under his *nón lá*, lost to the world around him.

Hội-An fisherman casting net on the river Thu-Bồn.

The boat soon pulls in at a large island. We clamber out onto a makeshift jetty and stare up at a huge sign atop two thick columns that welcomes visitors to "Làng Mộc Kim-Bồng," the carpentry village of Kim-Bồng. According to Trí, for the past five centuries village artisans, who originated from the north, have earned a great reputation working on furniture and houses all across the country, from Hà-Nội to the imperial city of Huế to Hội-An in its heyday. Yet despite its fame, Kim-Bồng looks no different from any other Vietnamese rural village. We amble past hedges of bougainvillea that enclose fruit or vegetable gardens and dirt yards where chickens and an occasional piglet forage next to one another. Tall, skinny betel-nut trees, of the palm family, sway gently in the sun—a lovely sight that has long been a cherished symbol of family, village, and tradition. Few people after my grand-parents' generation still chew the betel nut anymore, but it continues to be used, together with the piper vine leaves, as offerings on the ancestral altar during important occasions like weddings or the traditional New Year's celebrations.

Trí takes us to visit a couple of shops, where we watch generational woodworkers ply their skillful art while squatting on the bare ground, which is littered with saw dust, mother-of-pearl flakes, and pans of lacquer. Their finished products—furniture, religious statues, crafted screens and doors, and a wide array of knickknacks—are on display in the shopfronts. Kim-Bồng is also known for its traditional boat-building, but unfortunately we've run out of time to tour any shipyard. On our way back to the jetty, we wander through the village market and I stop at a souvenir stall to buy some trinkets from a mother and her little girl.

The boat returns to the Hội-An pier where the bus is expecting us. The temperature isn't intolerable but the humidity has grown quite oppressive. We all heave a sigh of relief as we escape into the air-conditioned coach. It feels heavenly.

"We'll be having lunch at another village, Trà-Quế, two miles from here," Trí announces after everyone has settled down. "The village specializes in organically grown vegetables and herbs, which it has been supplying to the greater Hội-An area for over three hundred years."

The farmers there fertilize their crops using a special kind of algae harvested from a nearby lagoon, and it's known to give their vegetables and herbs their famous texture and flavor. The village's pride in its agrarian tradition is obvious since its composite name was derived from a special herb—tea (*trà*)—and a spice, cinnamon (*quế*).

The bus follows a two-lane road out of town, soon driving through beautiful countryside dotted with rice fields against a backdrop of mountains and river. Here and there, a water buffalo ruminates contentedly along the muddy embankment, while another waddles behind its owner in his conical hat, no doubt on the way to their next task. Before long, the motor coach slows down, turns off onto a narrow lane for a short distance, then pulls over to a complete stop.

"We have to walk in from here, but not very far," says Trí as we get off the bus. "Please be careful. Don't block the road, and watch out for motor scooters from both directions."

Trà-Quế, being on the mainland and close to the town, seems more urbanized than Kim-Bồng, as evidenced by brick houses with tile roofs that line the half-paved lane. Also, in recent years the village has become a favorite stop for tourists, who travel here in busloads to admire its idyllic setting and vegetable gardens and to observe its inhabitants' simple, healthy lifestyle. As such, it has grown to enjoy a previously unknown level of prosperity.

Past the residential area, on both sides of the road lie large fields of the popular herbs and vegetables. Neatly organized into luxuriant-looking plots and rows of various sizes, they form a giant checkerboard of soothing shades of green and yellow. We turn onto a dirt path that cuts to the middle of the nearest field and arrive at our lunch destination: an open-air hut with a quaint dining area, shielded from the element by a thatch roof set on bamboo posts.

"Our meal will be prepared with the freshest ingredients right off the field," Trí says. "But first, you get to learn how to make Hội-An's famous sizzling cakes, or *bánh xèo.*"

We gather around the cooking station and watch a young chef in white hat and apron show off his teppanyaki-like skills—heating the frying pan over high flames, pouring into it the flour mix and chopped-up ingredients that spark and crackle, then flipping the crepe high in the air at the exact right time, all carried out with flashy showmanship and hilarious commentaries. Those brave souls among us who wish to try their hands at making their own *bánh xèo* get a chance to do so under the watchful eye of the "tyrannical" young chef. Then after all the fun and laughter that leaves everyone exhilarated but starving, we sit down to a meal as grand and delicious as any we've had on the trip. I lose track of how many sizzling cakes, served up with the crunchiest vegetables and a mouthwatering dip, I actually devour.

After lunch, happily sated, we amble back across the field to the village road and follow it out to the bus. The day excursion now over, the driver is taking us back to the hotel, passing by Old Town on the way. It's only mid-afternoon and I'm tempted to ask if he can drop me off there, but in the end I decide not to. The heat and dripping humidity have succeeded in wearing me out after our fun day, and since we're leaving in the morning, I also need to pick up my washed laundry from across the street and start packing—again.

Hội-An viewed from the river.

Overnight the stifling mugginess turns into rain; a steady drizzle that threatens to get worse, if the leaden sky above is any indicator.

We check out after breakfast and then, covering our heads with hats and umbrellas, dash out to the bus to begin boarding. Settling into our seats, dry and cozy, we await departure as soon as the porter finishes loading the luggage. Suddenly, out of the blurry window, I see him. An old man—a double amputee—in his wheelchair, wrapped in a green hooded raincoat with a floppy hat over the hood, smiling up at us from the wet street while waving a folding umbrella for sale, with many more stored in a clear plastic bag he is holding in his lap. His face is weathered and deeply lined, his smile hopeful and toothless. It occurs to me that he might be a veteran from the former South Vietnamese army, one of countless "losers" in the cruel game of war, now struggling to survive on the fringe of society. I search in my pockets and take out what money bills I can find, then rush off the bus to give them to the man. His eyes, smiling at me up close, are faded and rheumy, from the years and the rain. He tries to hand me the umbrella, but I shake my head—No, thank you, you keep it. But the words won't come, so choked up am I with emotion. I manage to nod at him before scrambling back to my seat.

As the bus rumbles, ready to take off, the man wheels away, his green shadow soon out of sight. The rain shows no sign of letting up, and the bus lumbers along in clogged traffic. On the wet and slippery sidewalk, a woman in *nón lá* and soaked raincoat bends under the hefty baskets on her shoulder pole, fighting to keep her balance with every step. It makes me wince to watch her weave around puddles, causing the baskets to swing and bobble precariously. A misstep would surely spell disaster for her and her family. But I imagine this is just a typical scene in the day-to-day struggle of the local people— real life playing out mere blocks away from the tourist hotspot. It fills me with sadness, a heavy feeling that matches the gloom outside. Then the bus moves on and, like the veteran in the wheelchair moments earlier, the unknown woman falls behind and quickly dwindles back into obscurity.

Outside Hội-An, we head back north toward Đà-Nẵng, which we'll be passing through on our way to Huế, the Imperial City. It's a distance of just under a hundred miles that takes about three hours to cover. But before we start out on the long stretch, Trí has planned a couple of stops for us, the first one being China Beach. We feel certain that luck is again on our side, since the rain has subsided somewhat. But no sooner does the bus pull over to let us out than the sky opens up again, sending us scurrying back to dry safety. We're in no way missing out on a great day at the beach, however, judging by the roiling ocean and the storm clouds.

Instead, we get to spend more time indoors at a stone-art shop further up the road, by Ngũ-Hành-Sơn, or Marble Mountains. It's a huge production center of stone products of all types—sculptures of various motifs and sizes, indoor and outdoor furniture, large and small decorative items, stone jewelry, etc.—all made from the local marble that comes in different colors. The prices on the tags of many of these exquisite items are staggering, so I'm happy to just browse around, admiring the impressive display or watching the artisans chipping at new blocks of stone.

By the time we leave the shop, the rain is getting heavier, finally coming down in sheets as we cross the Dragon Bridge over the Hàn River and arrive in downtown Đà-Nẵng. I suspect Trí has hoped to give us a tour of the renovated city center because the bus route takes us right past new, flashy buildings and manicured parks. Unfortunately, it's pouring so hard by now we can scarcely see out the streaky windows. What jumps out at me, though, is how badly flooded all the streets are, which indicates that the sewer system is in dire need of updating. As I watch motor-scooter riders navigate the rushing streams that the streets have turned into, I'm reminded of the constant danger the monsoon poses to the Central Coast: At any time, a severe storm can trigger mudslides or flooding that wreak havoc and even death. From the earliest beginnings, the resilient natives have had to cope with seasonal rain as both a blessing that brings life to this otherwise arid region and a recurring curse that threatens to destroy everything in its path.

The bus splashes ahead, lulling us into silence. Everyone seems hypnotized by the rain and is probably pondering how fortunate we were yesterday to have escaped this downpour. There is little doubt it would have wiped out the entire day and left us with a soggy memory of Hội-An.

And what a shame and terrible loss that would have been.

Chapter Three

On the Perfume River

Tuesday, November 8

As the bus leaves the flooded streets of Đà-Nẵng behind and trundles north on Quốc-Lộ Một (National Route One), heavy rain continues to dog us. Soon the road begins to climb toward Hải-Vân Pass, renowned for its scenic beauty as well as its treacherous mountain drive. I can't help but wonder how dangerous the crossing may be in these weather conditions.

The pass, where low clouds often mingle with rising sea mist (hence its name, which means "ocean clouds"), straddles a spur of the Trường-Sơn Range that juts into the South China Sea. A natural rampart of major strategic importance, it once formed the boundary between Việt-Nam and Champa that was subsequently pushed south to the Thu-Bồn River. The pass also marks the dividing barrier between the northern and southern climates such that at any given moment Huế and Đà-Nẵng, although just 70 miles apart, may experience drastically different weather.

As if guessing my concerns, Trí makes an announcement over the speaker. "Okay. We are about to enter the Hải-Vân Tunnel under the pass. This is much safer and faster than trying to cross over it, especially in nasty weather like this. The tunnel was built by Japanese and Korean contractors and opened to traffic in 2005. It only has two lanes now, which will be expanded to four in the near future. It is also the longest tunnel in Southeast Asia, at just under four miles."

I breathe in relief as the bus plunges into the well-lit tunnel, emerging on the northern end after only 10 minutes—a trip that according to Trí could take anywhere from 45 to 90 minutes should one opt for the twisting road over the pass. Further north along the coastline, I get the feeling we've arrived into a new locale. The earlier downpour, blocked by the Hải-Vân Pass, has thinned to a drizzle, allowing patches of blue to break through in the sky. If our luck continues to hold, the weather should clear up by the time we reach Huế.

Huế. My stomach flutters with excitement at the thought of the ancient capital. Even though it's a relatively small city with a population of 400,000, Huế has always held a special place in the hearts of the Vietnamese people, not merely as our foremost historical and cultural center but also as a destination of unique beauty. Wedged between scenic mountains, lakes and lagoons, and the famous Perfume River, the city was founded in the 17th century and has since occupied a prominent position in the country's history. Known in the early days by its original name, Phú-Xuân, it served as the seat of power for the Nguyễn lords over its first 200 years. Then, in 1802, after centuries of civil war, the country was unified under the Nguyễn Dynasty and Huế became the new imperial capital of Việt-Nam. It retained that status until 1945, when the dynasty collapsed. Throughout the 1945–1954 Independence War against the French and the Việt-Nam War in the 1960s and '70s, the city suffered a great deal of mayhem and destruction. I still remember as a kid watching with my parents the TV news about the horrors befalling Huế and her citizens during the Tết Offensive in 1968—images I'll never forget.

The road soon cuts through an urbanized area that grows denser by the minute with modest-looking houses, storefronts, and market. A large sign points to nearby Phú-Bài International Airport, and with a start I realize we're almost at the city limits. Located 10 miles south of Huế, Phú-Bài is a major airport that played an important role during the war, having hosted in turn a U.S. Marine Corps base, the 85th Evacuation Hospital, the headquarters of the 101st Airborne Division, and a South Vietnamese logistics base.

From Phú-Bài it takes another half hour before we get to the city—the "modern" section outside the Citadel walls, on the south bank of the river. Through narrow streets that bustle with activity, we arrive at our hotel—a compound of two buildings in the sixties style, four and six stories high respectively, fronted by a wide driveway and a lush garden with big trees. The buildings are painted in white and appear freshly renovated. In between them, I glimpse the Perfume River at the back of the hotel, a glistening ribbon under the hazy sun.

Inside the lobby decorated with wood carving panels that depict scenes within the Imperial City, a woman dressed in the traditional *áo dài* welcomes us and proceeds to check us in.

"It's now noon. Let's meet back here in two hours," says Trí after we've all received our room keys. "You can grab lunch here at the hotel or check out the restaurants across the street. We are visiting the Citadel this afternoon. Lots to see, and we just barely have enough time."

It turns out the Citadel—the fortified ancient capital—lies on the north bank of the river almost directly across from the hotel. Constructed according to the geomancy rules of Eastern tradition combined with the defense principles championed by Sébastien de Vauban, France's foremost military architect under Louis XIV, this unusual fortress has a square shape of 1.5 miles on each side. It consists of three distinct cities laid out in concentric enclosures: the Capital, Imperial, and Forbidden Purple Cities, each with its own wall. The result is an elegant complex of palaces and temples protected by massive ramparts, bastions, and moats. Together with other monuments in the picturesque surrounding areas, the Citadel was cited as "a masterpiece of urban poetry" and inscribed on the World Heritage List in 1993 by UNESCO.

As planned, after lunch the bus drives us across the neighboring Tràng-Tiền Bridge into the Old Capital. This quarter-mile steel-and-concrete bridge was built in 1899-1900, the oldest of its kind in Việt-Nam, and has since become a familiar fixture of the Huế scenery. From this point on, I'm fully prepared to get bombarded with names at every turn—familiar names I had learned at an early age from history and literature books or picked up from the news, names that go back many centuries, an intrinsic part of our heritage.

After crossing the bridge, the bus turns west and rolls slowly along the riverbank, parallel to a wide moat and a huge stone wall that encircle the whole capital. According to my travel notes, the rampart measures 22 feet high and 70 feet thick and is defended by no less than 24 bastions distributed around its periphery. Entrance into the Citadel is controlled through 10 imposing gates surmounted by double-story watchtowers. The bus skips the first such gate right after the bridge, Cửa Thượng-Tứ, and deposits us in front of the next one.

"Buses are not allowed inside; we have to walk from here," says Trí, leading us off the big coach. "Please stay close to the curb. Cửa Thế-Nhân is a very busy gate, with a lot of traffic."

My feet suddenly seem to possess a mind of their own, propelling me past Trí and our tour group, across the paved bridge over the moat and headlong into the tunnel-like gateway under the watchtower. It takes my breath away to think I'm only a few steps from entering this ancient city, which I've loved all my life without ever having set foot in it, and about to take a stroll back in history among its monuments and ruins. I hear Trí's voice in my wireless earbuds, "Parts of the wall and many of these gates were heavily damaged during the war, but they have all been restored, so you now see them as they appeared two hundred years ago."

Emerging from the entryway, I stumble onto a grassy esplanade that looks immense under billowing dark clouds. We're so fortunate it hasn't rained, but the mugginess is palpable. I feel my shirt sticking to my back. The group catches up behind me, and Trí resumes his explanation.

"Immediately to our right are four of Cửu Thần-Công, or the Nine Deities Cannons, cast in bronze by order of Emperor Gia-Long in 1803 as symbolic protection for his new capital. These four were named after the seasons. As for the other five"—he pivots left and points across the open grounds—"see the flag tower out there in the middle? The remaining five cannons have been moved to the gate on the other side of the tower. They are said to represent the five classic elements: metal, wood, water, fire, and earth." Without interrupting his talk, Trí follows the walking path around the esplanade in the direction of the tower, with us on his heels. "The Flag Tower sits atop a three-tiered pyramid, and the staff itself is seventy feet tall and made of concrete. Yeah . . . back in the days, a giant imperial flag in yellow velvet or brocade with a dragon design in its center would fly on ceremonial occasions. It could be spotted from miles away."

I've just finished snapping a picture when, out of the corner of my eye, I catch a glimpse of it, set back from the expansive grounds and directly facing the flag tower—the most celebrated sight of Huế, featured in countless photographs in books and magazines.

"And here we are," announces Trí with a sweep of his hand, "at Cửa Ngọ Môn, the Gate of Noon. It's the main entrance to Đại-Nội, which means the Great Enclosure—the Imperial City."

Cửa Ngọ Môn (Gate of Noon): Entrance to Đại-Nội (Imperial City).

The Imperial City is a square of half a mile on each side, ringed by a moat with 10 bridges and by a rampart of its own, which measures 13 feet high and 3 feet thick. It once served as the seat of government and also includes the Forbidden Purple City, the emperor's private domain. Access can be gained through four gates, but Cửa Ngọ Môn was strictly limited for use by the emperor and the court. Of the three entrances in this gate, the middle one with red lacquered doors was reserved for the emperor only. It is the widest and tallest in order to accommodate the imperial elephants. Atop the 17-foot stone gate rises the splendid, double-story Ngũ-Phụng Lâu, or Pavilion of Five Phoenixes; named, it is said, due to its resemblance, when viewed from above, to a group of five of the mythical birds with beaks joining and wings widespread. From this vantage point, the emperor sat enthroned to preside over important state occasions.

Passing through the Gate of Noon, we come out onto Trung-Đạo (Middle Path) Bridge, a spacious walkway that runs up the central axis of the Citadel and spans the lotus-filled Thái-Dịch (Great Water) Lake. Through a pair of portals erected on bronze columns sculpted with dragons, the bridge leads up to the Great Rites Court (Sân

Đại-Triều) and, beyond it, the most significant building in the Imperial City, the Hall of Supreme Harmony (Điện Thái-Hoà).

Also known as the Throne Palace, Điện Thái-Hoà is a magnificent hall dominated by 80 red-lacquered ironwood columns entwined with gilded dragons. Its massive roof is decked in yellow glazed ceramic tiles and adorned with nine dragons. The palace provided a formal setting for such major state affairs as coronations, royal birthdays, bi-monthly Great Audiences, receptions of foreign emissaries, etc. On these occasions, the emperor would sit in resplendent regalia—dragon crown, gold robe, jade belt—on his elevated throne in the center of the hall. Only the four most senior mandarins were allowed inside the hall, while others stood outside in the stone-paved Great Rites Court—civil mandarins to the left and military to the right—lined up in their appointed places on the upper or lower terrace according to their ranks.

Across Trung-Đạo Bridge to Điện Thái-Hòa (Hall of Supreme Harmony).

By this time, I'm bringing up the rear of the group, in part intention-ally because I want to wait for the crowd to clear out before I take my photos. Treading lightly, out of respect, through the Hall of Supreme Harmony, I rush out the back door and down a flight of stone steps guided by dragon balustrades to catch up with the group. We find ourselves in a sprawling courtyard that stretches to a single long wall in the far back. The wall is in a sad state of dilapidation, covered with black grime. Ringing the sides of the empty courtyard are two identical L-shaped structures, the Halls of the Mandarins. Tả-Vu on the left was reserved for civil and Hữu-Vu on the right for military mandarins.

Trí motions at the vast open space around us. "Much of the Imperial City was destroyed during the war—razed to the ground. Yeah . . . that's why it looks so empty, almost like a ghost town in some parts— right in here, for instance. Everything that we see today has been carefully restored, but there's still a lot of work left to be done. It will take years to finish."

In fact, during the celebration of Tết (the Vietnamese New Year) in 1968, the Communists breached the ceasefire and took Huế by surprise, occupying it for 25 days. As the South Vietnamese and U.S. troops mounted a counteroffensive to retake the city, the Communist army retreated inside the Citadel, where the final battle caused substantial casualties and damage. In the end, out of 160 historic buildings within the Imperial and Forbidden Cities, just 10 remained standing in various states of ruin. Fortunately, many are being restored or reconstructed with the assistance of international experts under the umbrella of UNESCO.

Trí ambles past the huge bronze cauldrons on display in front of the Halls of the Mandarins. "In the old days, the mandarins would use these halls to prepare for audiences with the emperor and other court ceremonies," he explains. "Let's just walk through Tả-Vu over here, which was reserved for civil mandarins. It's now used to showcase rare photographs and imperial articles."

I've also read that these halls once served as the site where *thi đình*, the court examinations, were held every three years to appoint future mandarins from the best and brightest in the nation. To sit for the prestigious *thi đình*, one must have already passed the rigorous regional (*thi hương*) and national (*thi hội*) examinations. This antiquated yet surprisingly democratic system was kept in place right up to my grandparents' generation, until it was abolished by the French in 1913. I vaguely remember old family lore from childhood about my mother's father—a young man at the time—having just taken and passed his regional examination when the thousand-year-old system became obsolete overnight. As I gaze at these hallowed halls, trying to imagine the solemn scene of a *thi đình* in centuries past, it touches me deeply to think that my forebear might once have aspired to such honors—before the old way of life vanished forever.

Exiting Tả-Vu, we follow Trí onto the raised platform that borders the lone wall at the end of the courtyard. Bedecked with imperial dragons along its top and flanked on either side by freshly renovated structures, the wall appears to have been blackened by char marks and grime.

"We're now standing on the foundation of Cần-Chánh Palace, which served as the working office of the emperor," says Trí. "It was in here that he held regular work meetings with the mandarins, aside from the formal Great Audiences in the Hall of Supreme Harmony. That's how this large courtyard acquired its name: Sân Bái-Đình, or the Court of Audiences."

The original palace, built in 1804, was aligned with other significant monuments (Gate of Noon, Trung-Đạo Bridge, Hall of Supreme Harmony) along the central axis of the Imperial City. Many edifices once surrounded it, but according to my research, the entire complex—with the exception of this battered wall—was burned down in 1947 during the War of Independence against the French. Only in recent years has the government initiated a full-scale reconstruction project in cooperation with a team of Japanese experts.

War destruction: Empty courtyard with crumbling wall (Cẩn-Chánh Palace).

Trí stops before a narrow doorway at one end of the wall. "We are about to enter Tử-Cấm-Thành, the Forbidden Purple City. Nobody but the emperor and his family was allowed beyond this point." He pauses before adding wistfully, "There used to be beautiful palaces and gardens behind this wall, fifty buildings in all, but again, most of them were destroyed during the wars. So don't be too disappointed if you don't find a whole lot to photograph in here."

Technically speaking, the Forbidden Purple City begins immediately after the Hall of Supreme Harmony, where an elaborate gate called Đại-Cung Môn (Grand Palace Gate) used to stand. The empty courtyard that we have just crossed, between the now-missing gate and the charred wall, was once the site of important offices—the nerve center of the government bureaucracy. The wall, a giant brick screen, separated this working area from the off-limits residences of the imperial family, collectively known as Càn-Thành Palace, after the majestic structure occupied by the emperor himself.

Following Trí and stumbling through the small doorway into the once-forbidden quarters, I instantly grasp what he was trying to tell us, as I gaze in dismay at a vast open space covered with grass and puddles of rainwater. Save for two symmetrical galleries running down the sides and a couple of buildings in the far back, the whole area lies naked and forsaken under the turbulent sky. Even the silence weighs heavy with nostalgia. We wander down the gallery to our right, a resplendent hallway draped in gild and red lacquer. It is so far the only reconstructed part of Quang-Minh Palace, which used to be the private residence of the Crown Prince.

Restored hallway in Quang-Minh Palace in the Forbidden City.

Since we are short on time, Trí decides to skip other notable buildings in the Forbidden City: the Imperial Theater, the Imperial Library, and the Queen Mothers' and Grand Queen Mothers' residences, all in various stages of restoration. Sidestepping the rain puddles, we cross the grass field and head back out through the long gallery on the other side, the reconstructed hallway of Trinh-Minh Palace, where high-ranking concubines once lived.

"I want to take you by the important shrines in the southwest corner before we leave," says Trí, as we exit the Forbidden City and follow a paved road along its 12-foot-high wall. My feet are now hurting and I'm drenched in sweat, but I'm so thankful we have been spared any rain, despite the threatening clouds. For how much sightseeing could we truly have enjoyed while bundled up in raincoats or wrestling with umbrellas in the driving monsoon?

At the end of the road, we turn away from the Forbidden City wall and file through an ornate gateway into the temples' area. A path leads us through a garden to a second gate, which opens onto a court dominated by the imposing Dynastic Temple, or Temple of Generations (Thế Miếu). This grand hall houses the altars of 10 of the 13 emperors of the Nguyễn Dynasty, starting in the center with the altar dedicated to Emperor Gia-Long, the dynasty founder. Taking advantage of the sun's breaking through, Trí proposes we all gather in front of the shrine for a group photo.

On the south side of the court, directly facing the Temple of Generations, is a classic three-tiered building with a distinguished pyramid shape: Hiển-Lâm Các, or the Pavilion of Everlasting Glory. Built entirely of wood as a memorial to those princes and mandarins who had contributed to the rise of the dynasty, it soared above all other structures within the Citadel, at 60 feet high. As a sign of respect, it was decreed that no constructions could rise higher than Hiển-Lâm Các.

The pavilion, which is the least damaged of all the monuments, is flanked by two beautiful gates that reflect its elegant style and combine to form a harmonious ensemble: On the left is the Gate of Great Heroes (Tuấn-Liệt Môn), topped by a belfry; and on the right is the Gate of Great Achievements (Sùng-Công Môn), surmounted with a drum tower. Together, the trio provides a perfect counterbalance to the Temple of Generations across the courtyard.

A row of gigantic bronze urns, weighing up to three tons each, lines the front of the pavilion. They are the Nine Dynastic Urns, or Cửu Đinh, cast in commemoration of nine emperors whose altars are located in the temple. Decorated with exquisite bas-reliefs of the sun, the moon, and the country's diverse scenery, flora, and fauna, the urns were positioned in the same order as the emperors' altars inside the temple, with the largest one in the center being set forward by 10 feet to honor Emperor Gia-Long, the dynasty founder. They've never been moved since their initial installation in 1837 and have miraculously survived through all the wars.

Hiển-Lâm Các (Pavilion of Everlasting Glory) and
Cửu Đinh (the Nine Dynastic Urns).

We leave the walled temple area through the main exit behind the pavilion. A massive three-way gate garnished with sculptures of mythical animals, Hiển-Hữu Môn, or the Gate of Glorious Assistance, towers over 30 feet high to control access to this devotional enclosure. By now, we're dead on our feet from the long day and the walking tour, and our heads are spinning with all the tidbits of history and culture. It's a good thing Trí has arranged to have the group picked up by passenger carts and delivered to a parking lot outside the Citadel where our bus awaits. Sighing with relief as we plop down on the seats of the air-conditioned coach, we all seem to agree that we have done all the walking we can for this day.

Back at the hotel, we have half an hour to wash up and change clothes before meeting back in the lobby for the evening program. "I recommend you wear long pants and long-sleeve shirts and rub on some insect repellent," Trí reminds us. "Yeah . . . the mosquitoes, they really come out at dark." Then, grinning, he quickly adds, "But no more walking. I promise."

Instead, waiting for us in the hotel's driveway is a long line of shiny cyclos (pronounced "sik-los") he has reserved to transport us, one person per vehicle, back into the Citadel (the civilian section) for our special dinner. A cyclo is a three-wheeled pedicab invented in French Indochina during the colonial times after a failed attempt to popularize the Chinese rickshaw. The customer rides comfortably in a covered seat that rests on the two front wheels, while the driver perches high on a bicycle seat mounted above the rear wheel. Some of my earliest and most fun memories were when I squeezed in next to my mom or my dad on a cyclo, out on errands run to some unknown destination far away from home—my first thrills of adventure.

Trí gives each of us a face mask to cover our nose and mouth. "To protect you from all the dust and exhaust fumes," he explains. "It's rush hour out there." Without thinking, I stuff mine in my back pocket, which soon proves to be a mistake.

One by one, the cyclos file out onto tree-lined Lê-Lợi Avenue that runs along the south bank of the river. Pushing and shoving our ways into the noisy, chaotic stream of motor scooters that press dangerously close against the pedicabs, we ride past, in succession, the old French Quarter; the University of Huế; the French-Colonial Saigon Morin Hotel, one of the oldest hotels in Việt-Nam (est. 1901); a large city park; and the famous Quốc-Học High School attended by many historic figures. A winding right turn takes us onto a bridge over the river, where a nice breeze sweeps away the stinging smog that reminds me of Los Angeles in the '80s.

Once across the river, the cyclos pass under an ancient gate and meander through the busy shopping district inside the Citadel. Lining the streets are boxy buildings three or four stories tall, with flat rooftops and narrow storefronts brightly signed and lit. Traffic here is just as jammed as south of the river, if not worse, due to the tight confines within the Old City. We eventually make it out of the commercial zone and into a residential area, passing through an open market along the way. By the time the cyclos drop us off at our final destination, a large but unassuming old house in a quiet neighborhood, twilight has turned into total darkness.

Trí gathers the troop in front of the small entrance gate. "The family who owns this house has lived in it for generations," he says. "Their ancestors used to serve in the Palace, preparing meals for the emperors, and they kept passing those traditions down to the next generation. So tonight the current owner has agreed to cook a special dinner for us as her guests. Yeah . . . it will include some of the imperial courses with all the fancy presentation that came with them."

The owner, a young-looking woman dressed in the traditional *áo dài*, welcomes us in English and gives us a tour of the ground floor, which is more like a museum packed with rare antiques and handicrafts. Afterward, she leads us through a small garden to a ranch-style building that serves as the banquet room, where we sit down to dinner. Even with the air conditioner and the fans on, it feels warm and stuffy, especially once the diligent waitresses start coming and going through the doors. I can also hear the mosquitoes buzzing around and am thankful I'd heeded Trí's warning and sprayed on insect repellent before we left.

The food is delicious, all the more since we're famished after the long day, but in my view no more extraordinary than the meals we've had at previous places. What's unique, however, is its elaborate presentation, which aims to delight and entertain: classic spring rolls stuck on a pared pineapple with colorful garnishes to emulate a pheasant's plumage; fried rice with egg strips and carved vegetables, arranged in the shape of a tortoise; fresh fruits peeled to look like open lotus flowers. Every time a new dish is brought out, camera flashes immediately go off around the tables as we hustle to snap pictures of the fanciful creation before devouring it. All in all, it's a perfect fun evening to cap off a whirlwind day of traveling and touring.

It's only nine o'clock by the time the bus brings us back to the hotel, but it feels much later to my tired body. And so I'm glad to be back in my room, which is decorated with a traditional Vietnamese flair that befits the historic location: bamboo-like furniture, embroidered bed scarf and pillow cases, and frosted glass with aquatic motifs. My last thoughts as I drift off to sleep are of my late parents, who lived in Huế for a few years in the '50s: Did they stay inside the Citadel or on the south bank? Were they as taken with our ancient capital as I am now? How hard a struggle was it for them, as a young couple with small children, to get by during wartime? And what made them later move to Đà-Nẵng, where I was born, and eventually to Sài-Gòn? I realize, belatedly and with sadness, that I don't really know much about my parents' early years.

The next morning I go down to the breakfast buffet in the cafeteria on the ground floor. Its wall of glass brings in a panoramic view of the river and the north bank that is spectacular. I can see clear to the Đông-Ba Market to the northeast, just outside the Citadel wall—the oldest and largest covered market in the city. After breakfast, on my way back to the elevator, I bump into a woman from our group who has just come back from her exploration walk around the hotel.

"Do you know," she says with wide eyes, "that this place used to be the Officers' Quarters of the South Vietnamese Army back in the days? It was attacked by the Communists during the Tết Offensive in 1968, and there's an encased bullet hole in the second floor's window to prove it." Then, shaking her head, "So much history at every corner. Amazing, isn't it?"

I promise her I'll check it out later, but right now I need to hurry to get my knapsack then join Trí and the rest of our group for the day excursion. As it is, I'm among the last stragglers to arrive at the rendezvous dock adjoining the cafeteria. We promptly board our "dragon boat," a motorboat whose bow is decked out in garish ornaments shaped like dragon heads, replete with scales, teeth, and whiskers. As the boat bounces away from the dock, heading west upstream, it appears we're lucking out on another propitious day—overcast and sultry, but still with no rain.

Trí's voice comes on the speaker over the engine noise and the splashing of waves. "You probably wonder how the Perfume River got its name, yeah? It came from the scented flowers of the frangipani, or plumeria, trees the emperors planted along the riverbanks. Also, in the autumn, flowers from orchards upriver fall into the water, and that gives it a wonderful fragrance."

Besides providing the lifeblood to the local agriculture and a water highway to the entire region, the river, with its scenic surroundings, has long been a source of inspiration to poets and artists of all stripes, among them many princes and emperors. Watching the lovely landscape flow by under a sky of drifting clouds, it's easy to imagine how, until just a couple of generations ago, a leisurely boat ride on a moonlit night (when the frangipani flowers are fully open and at their most fragrant), accompanied with wine, food, live music, and poetry, would be deemed a genteel and romantic way to spend an evening.

On the north bank, right outside the Citadel wall in front of the Flag Tower, stand two structures that look like miniature pagodas but loom large in historical significance. The first one is Phu-Văn Lâu, or the Pavilion of Edicts, where imperial edicts and the lists of successful candidates of *thi hội* and *thi đình* (the national and court examinations) were posted. As a mark of respect, two stone steles erected on either side of the pavilion reminded people to "tilt your hats and dismount" when passing by the monument. In 1916, two nationalists disguised as fishermen met in secret with Emperor Duy-Tân at Phu-Văn Lâu to plot an uprising against the French. The mission unfortunately failed; the nationalists were captured and beheaded, and the patriotic 16-year-old emperor was deposed and exiled to Reunion Island in the Indian Ocean.

A wide paved court connects Phu-Văn Lâu to Nghênh-Lương Đình, or the Pavilion for Fresh Breeze, by the river. This was known as the best vista point in the capital from which the emperor could admire the river scenery at sunrise, sunset, or on a moonlit night. From there, 13 steps lead down to the water where the dragon boat would have been moored, waiting for him.

Distracted by all the tourist-carrying boats racing around us, I forget to look out for these historic monuments—whose images are imprinted on the backside of the 50,000-*đồng* bill—until we've long passed them and the Flag Tower. Instead, squinting against reflected sunlight, all I'm able to glimpse is a small herd of docile water buffalo cooling themselves off by the riverbank, totally submerged except for their long, curved horns.

About two miles southwest of the Citadel, we dock in at the foot of a pine-forested hill on the north bank, which is crowned by a seven-story octagonal tower. Climbing two long flights of steps to reach the 70-foot-tall tower, known as Tháp Phước-Duyên (Source of Happiness Tower), we arrive at the most iconic shrine in all of Huế, if not in all of Việt-Nam: the Pagoda of Thiên-Mụ (Celestial Lady). Long ago, according to local legend, an old lady appeared on this hill and prophesized that a king would come and erect a temple here to pray for peace and prosperity for the country. Upon hearing about it, Lord Nguyễn Hoàng authorized construction of the pagoda in 1601. Ever since then, it has been continuously maintained and on occasion expanded, with its most striking feature, Tháp Phước-Duyên, added on in 1844 by Emperor Thiệu-Trị.

Thiên-Mụ Pagoda over the Perfume River.

Flanking the tower, whose seven stories symbolize the seven stages of enlightenment in Buddhism, are two hexagonal pavilions. One of them shelters an eight-foot stone stele riding on the back of a marble tortoise (ca. 1715), and the other a huge bronze bell called Đại Hồng Chung, eight feet tall and weighing over three tons. The bell was cast in 1710, and its toll can be heard for miles around. Beyond, colorful and larger-than-life sculptures of fearsome deities stand guard at a three-way entrance that leads into a beautiful courtyard; the main temple, Đại-Hùng (Great Hero) Shrine; other worship halls; and facilities for residing bonzes. The sweeping view of mountains and river from this hilltop is breathtaking, almost otherworldly. It complements to perfection the noble architecture and the long, rich history to make Thiên-Mụ Pagoda the defining landmark of Huế, immortalized in literature, music, and folk rhymes (*ca dao*).

Back at the bottom of the hill, we are picked up by the bus, which then crosses back over the river to the south bank. After a 20-minute drive through sparsely populated areas, it deposits us at the entrance to the mausoleum of Emperor Tự-Đức. Although 13 rulers sat on the imperial throne between 1802 and 1945, only seven were buried in their own mausoleums (or *lăng*) around the capital. Of those seven Royal Tombs, which together with the Old Citadel form Huế's greatest attraction, this one, dedicated to the fourth emperor, is the largest and considered by many the most exquisitely designed. Built in a valley within a pine forest, it initially served as the emperor's favorite retreat during the remainder of his lifetime. The walled enclosure, set amidst fragrant pines and frangipani trees and dotted with tranquil ponds, includes no less than 50 structures of various sizes. Their names all contain the term "Khiêm" (Humility) to express the emperor's belated remorse for having burdened his people with such a grandiose construction project. The mausoleum itself has come to be known as Khiêm Lăng.

Past the main entrance at Vụ-Khiêm Gate, we amble along the shore of a lake-stream where a pair of pavilions rises out of the water like lotus flowers. I instantly recognize this beloved vista of Khiêm Lăng, which captures so well the natural beauty and serenity it's famous for. Directly above the lake, we scale two flights of stone steps and arrive at Khiêm-Cung Môn, the majestic three-way, double-story entry gate to the walled compound of palaces and temples. The emperor and his entourage of concubines and mandarins used to stay here when they came out from the Citadel, so the compound also includes work offices and a royal theater, one of the oldest in the country. After his death in 1883 at the age of 54, most of these buildings were converted into funerary halls to house the altars of the emperor, his wives, and the Queen Mother Từ-Dụ.

Next to the palatial compound, and sloping uphill, is the tomb area proper. Passing through a gate at the end of a shady walk, we climb more steps and reach the wide Court of Audiences (Bái Đình), with a guard of stone elephants, horses, and diminutive mandarins. Beyond these rows of honor stands the Stele Pavilion (Bi Đình), which shelters a stone tablet 13 feet high, 7 feet wide, and 2 feet thick, and weighing 20 tons—the largest of its kind in Việt-Nam. The stele carries the inscription of Tự-Đức's epitaph, drafted—with unusual candor— by the emperor himself, since he had no children of his own. A tiny lagoon in half-moon shape separates the pavilion from the walled sepulcher, Bửu Thành, at the top of the hill. Here, under the singing pines, lie in eternal rest the emperor; his primary wife, the empress; and his adopted son, the emperor Kiến-Phúc. It was rumored, however, that Tự-Đức's body was actually interred at a secret site elsewhere.

Mausoleum of Emperor Tự-Đức (Xung-Khiêm Pavilion on Lưu-Khiêm Lake).

"Are you all hungry yet? We will be taking our lunch break at a Buddhist temple nearby," Trí announces as we circle back to the main entrance. "But first, one quick stop on the way."

The bus drops us off at a small workshop along the dusty roadside. It's not much more than a shack that is wide open on three sides, but under its tin roof we get to watch, up close, women workers in the process of making incense sticks and palm-leaf conical hats (*nón lá*). Some of the hats are decorated with pretty images or even with lines of verse inserted between the layers of leaf, patterns that distinctly show when the hats are held up to sunlight. I'm excited to see with my own eyes these so-called "poem hats," or *nón bài thơ*, an original product of Huế.

A stone's throw from the shop, hidden away on a dirt path off the main road, is our lunch destination: a surprisingly impressive and new-looking pagoda, with double stories and an ornate roof. It just seems to materialize out of thin air in the middle of the rural area.

"This is an abbey for Buddhist nuns," says Trí as we mount a breezy stairway to the dining hall on the second floor. "One of the ways they support themselves is by providing fresh, healthy vegetarian meals to tour groups like us. I hope you'll enjoy our lunch here."

It turns out to be a delicious treat—light and wholesome, yet quite tasty—and it really hits the spot after a long, hot morning. I overhear somebody at the next table declare in a contented voice, "Boy, if this is what vegetarian tastes like, you can sign me up anytime."

After lunch, with Trí serving as her interpreter, a young apprentice nun graciously offers to answer any questions we may have about life at the monastery. Then the head nun invites us to visit the worship hall just across the way, where we are welcome to light a stick of incense and pray, if we so wish. The high-ceilinged hall, dominated by an imposing bronze statue of Buddha on the altar, feels cool from the ceramic tiles on the floor. As we wander through it, I notice a teenage boy poking his head in from the front veranda. He has a sweet, albeit half-bewildered smile on his face and carries a bunch of handheld fans, which he shows to us without a word as we pass by him. I figure he must be a kid in the neighborhood, maybe with some mental deficiency, whom the nuns have allowed in to sell a few trinkets. Some of us stop and give the boy money without taking a fan in return, which seems to confuse him. So I nod and smile to reassure him that all is well, but I can't help but wonder how kids with such challenges manage to get by in this transitional society—or if they're not simply allowed to slip through the cracks.

After thanking the nuns for their hospitality, we take leave of them and get back on the bus, heading to the last sight on today's itinerary: the mausoleum of Khải-Định, the twelfth and next-to-last Nguyễn emperor, also the least popular during his lifetime due to his close collaboration with the French. Built between 1920 and 1931 into the slope of Châu-Chữ Mountain, about four miles southwest of Emperor Tự-Đức's resting place, this is the smallest, yet the most elaborate, of all the Royal Tombs. It also stands out as a unique fusion of different architectural styles: Asian and European, as well as traditional and modern, down to the materials used.

The tomb has a rectangular layout that reclines against the slope in three main levels, which are accessed by 127 steps from bottom to top. As we slowly scale the first triple-wide stairway with four concrete banisters adorned with dragons, the largest such sculptures in Việt-Nam, the thought crosses my mind that it might have been wise if we'd made this our first visit of the day instead of the last one. At the top of the landing, we pause to catch our breath before entering through a massive wrought-iron gate supported by Indian-style columns. Crossing to the end of the terrace, which is bordered by a small building on each side—the Houses of the Mandarins—we arrive at yet another wide stairway. This one ascends to a more traditional portal that opens onto the Court of Audiences. Here, two double rows of stone elephants, horses, soldiers, and mandarins stand in homage, leading to the Stele Pavilion in the center. This octagonal structure, built in reinforced concrete and supported by Romanesque-style pillars and arches, houses the epitaph tablet. Flanking the pavilion is a pair of towers reminiscent of the ones found in Buddhist temples. From the Court, dragging ourselves up even more stairways, we finally reach the altar complex at the top, also known as Thiên-Định (Providence's Will) Palace.

Court of Audiences at the mausoleum of Emperor Khải-Định.

The complex consists of the Right and Left Guards' Chambers and, in the middle, Khải-Thành Temple. The emperor's altar with his portrait photograph is located in the temple's front hall, whose walls are decorated with rich mosaics of glass and porcelain. The floor is covered by enameled tiles with floral patterns, and the ceiling features a spectacular fresco deemed a national treasure that depicts nine dragons hiding in clouds. In the back hall, under the royal canopy, a bronze life-sized statue of Khải-Định in imperial regalia stares into eternity. The tomb itself lies 60 feet underneath the throne dais, which is ornamented with a bursting sun symbolizing the emperor's death. Overhead, the splendid canopy appears to be made of lacy brocade that almost seems to flutter, so I'm surprised to learn that it is actually carved and painted concrete that weighs over a ton.

Needing some fresh air, I escape out to the terrace in front of Khải-Thành Temple in time to catch the rising afternoon breeze. The bird's eye view from up here is stunning—so green and lush all around it's hard to believe we're only a few miles from the city. This, combined with the opulent originality of the monument, truly dazzles. It's no wonder this place has become one of the popular tourist stops in Huế, according to Trí. But in an odd kind of way, it also triggers the memory of a world-renowned attraction on the other side of the earth, despite obvious differences between the two: Neuschwanstein Castle in Bavaria, Germany. For both these lavish constructions were built on a rugged hillside amidst an idyllic setting, with no costs spared; both born from the dreams of grandeur of self-indulgent monarchs who remained oblivious to their peoples' plights. In Khải-Định's case, in order to fund his extravagant project that took 10 years to complete—ironically, not until after his premature death—the emperor obtained permission from the French to increase taxes by 30%, which explained in part his great unpopularity.

Our group has now straggled out onto the terrace, and we begin our slow descent behind Trí, who is brandishing his guide's stick above his head as usual. As we pass the honor guard on the Court of Audiences, I hear commotion behind me and turn to see a few people dashing around with cell phones in hand, some pumping their fists in excitement, others with concern painted all over their faces. "What's going on back there?" I ask the woman next to me.

"Election results have been coming in back home," she whispers. "Sounds like Trump is well ahead of Clinton in electoral votes." Then, rolling her eyes and sighing, "We've got many supporters of both camps in our group. Real passionate they are, too. I just hope they don't get in each other's faces now. It sure would spoil the rest of the trip for all of us."

At the bottom of the hill, our faithful driver greets us with a smile as we clamber onto the bus. Trí, thoughtful as always, waits until we have all slid into our seats to announce the news, which he apparently assumes we're dying to learn. "Well, our driver says it is official now," he declares, nodding. "He has been following the news on his cell phone all afternoon. CNN has just called the election for Trump. Yeah . . . Trump won."

I must hand it to our group. The restraint shown by everyone is remarkable, as silence—tense silence, but silence nonetheless— descends on the bus. No outburst of frustration. No gleeful celebration. Just a few sighs and grumbles, and excited whispers. After a packed day, we're all feeling it, and nobody seems in the mood to throw a tantrum or do a victory dance. Nor, I suspect, does it hurt to have 8,000 miles of ocean between us and the political epicenter, where all hell must be breaking loose right this moment.

Back at the hotel driveway, as soon as the door wheezes open, we lumber off the bus and quickly disperse. I have no doubt they're all rushing back to their room to catch the latest TV reports and give vent to their emotions—all in private. And since we happen to have this last evening in Huế to ourselves, people can stay in and watch the news for as long as they like.

After washing off the sweat and dirt from the day, I cross the street in front of the hotel and grab dinner at a mom-and-pop restaurant. My mind isn't quite on the food; it keeps rewinding back to the scenes and events of the past 48 hours. Even though such a short visit can't possibly do justice to Huế, I'm thankful for all the sightseeing we've managed to take in. Despite its being my first trip to the city, I've instantly felt at home among the monuments and ruins, and with the historic names and anecdotes, the food, the people, and even the temperamental weather—as if I had lived here all my life. The exposure, however brief and sketchy, was sufficient to immerse me back in the history of my ancestral homeland, in a way that no books or movies can.

As I dart around rush-hour traffic, heading back to the hotel after dinner, it suddenly dawns on me: My lifelong fascination with Huế might have been what prompted me to make Elise, the beautiful piano player in *Once upon a Mulberry Field*, a daughter of the city: lovely and tragic, perpetually caught in the swirl of history, but resilient— like the city itself.

One way or another, I tell myself, I shall return to this special place for at least another visit. For this next trip, however, I will give myself plenty of time so I can adequately explore the history hidden in plain sight at every corner.

Chapter Four

Descending Dragon

Thursday, November 10

After an early breakfast, we check out of the hotel and promptly board the bus for a ride to Phú-Bài International Airport, 10 miles south of Huế. From there, we are to catch a flight to Hà-Nội, 420 miles to the north, or roughly a one-hour trip by air, where a new bus will be waiting to drive us to Hạ-Long Bay, our next destination.

Phú-Bài, despite its well-known military history during the Việt-Nam War and its current international status, feels more like a regional airport. The single terminal, while still retaining its original low-profile structure, has been given a complete makeover to bring it up to modern standards. As with previous domestic flights, we walk out on the tarmac to board the airplane.

Nội-Bài International Airport in Hà-Nội, on the other hand, is relatively new, only opened for business since 1978 as the postwar replacement for the outdated Gia-Lâm Airport. With two runways and two terminals, it's now the second busiest airport in the country, behind Tân-Sơn-Nhất in the south. We arrive around noontime at its domestic terminal, which I'm impressed to find as spacious and modern as its counterpart in Sài-Gòn.

After we've collected our luggage and completed our transfer to the new bus, Trí catches us up on the day's plan: "We are bypassing the city for now and driving straight to Hạ-Long Bay. It is one hundred and twenty-some miles from here, but the road is not so good and there's a lot of tourist traffic, so it will take about four hours. Yeah . . . it's pretty bad. I'm sorry about that. But we will make a stop at mid-point for a lunch and restroom break."

Watching the road through the window, I understand what he means. It's a rundown four-lane in need of repair on numerous stretches, which in turn explains the ongoing roadwork and continuous traffic jam. Crowded in on both sides by villages and townships, it has little room to expand to adequately accommodate swelling tourist transportation. Further adding to the traveling time is an obligatory stop at a tollbooth.

About 90 minutes into the trip, we reach Chí-Linh District in the province of Hải-Dương. I sit up like a shot when I sight the famous name on address signs along the road. This district was home to national hero Trần Hưng Đạo, who defeated the Mongols in 13th-century naval battles on the nearby rivers Lục-Đầu and Bạch-Đằng. It was also here where, 200 years later, statesman Nguyễn Trãi retired after helping to free Việt-Nam from Chinese rule under the Ming Dynasty. These great achievements rank among the most significant events in our history, which we all studied in school as kids. To this day, I've read, local festivals are still held annually at centuries-old temples to honor these heroes. In 1980, on the occasion of his 600th birthday, Nguyễn Trãi was recognized by UNESCO as a world cultural activist and statesman. With such illustrious sons and tradition, Chí-Linh has held a special place in the annals of Vietnamese history and has captured my imagination since early on, as a young boy fascinated with tales of valor. It fills me with awe that we're actually rolling through the heart of this historic land.

The bus slows down before turning off the road into a large parking lot next to a group of low buildings. Trí's voice comes on the speaker. "This is a work center established in the nineties to provide training in handicraft arts to young people with disabilities. It has been very successful and has expanded to include a restaurant in the back. So how about we go eat first, and then you can spend some time to browse and shop?"

Since it's long past lunch hour, we're the only tourist group in the diner and get attended to without delay. The food isn't bad for a roadside stop, and after finishing our meals, we dash over to the adjoining shop to explore. It's in a vast building that combines workshop, display room, and convenience store, all under one roof. Visitors are free to roam around and watch the young workers plying their craft, mainly hand embroidery, or examine the beautiful finished products that are hung on walls or displayed on tables around the floor. The prices are a bit higher than I expect, but the quality is excellent—and it's all for a good cause.

Workshop for underprivileged youths.

From the helpful sales clerks, I learn that the center has been in operation for almost 20 years and has benefited from its location on the highly traveled route. By cleverly offering the conveniences of a restaurant and clean restrooms in addition to the souvenir shop attraction, it has become a must stop along the road to Hạ-Long Bay. Another boon to tourism and commerce derives from a nearby 27-hole golf course that opened in 2003 and six years later was voted the most beautiful golf course in Việt-Nam. With such a favorable business climate, sales profits at the center are reinvested into growth expansion and building dormitories for apprentice students from afar.

Well-fed and invigorated from the needed break and toting bags of exquisite handicrafts whose sales proceeds go to support a worthwhile cause, we're all smiles as we climb back on the bus to resume our trip. It's more of the same road—narrow, dilapidated, and dusty, crawling with tour coaches that rumble their way through swarms of motor scooters—for another two hours before we spot the first welcome signs to Hạ-Long City in the late sunlight.

Until now, I've always thought of Hạ-Long in terms of its humble past—as a quiet fishing village situated on a bay of unsurpassed beauty—and have wondered how a place like that could accommodate the mobs of tourists descending upon it. The unequivocal answer lies straight ahead of us, along the broad avenue that leads into town where high rise after gleaming high rise soars into the sunset sky. Nowhere in sight is the old fishing village. It appears the new era of tourism has swooped it up and plunked down in its place another city with bright lights. "Miami Beach all over again," someone comments with a soft whistle.

"Ah, but these hotels are not doing as great as you may think," says Trí in response. "They get stiff competition from cruise-tours that offer overnight stay on their boats." He raises his hand to fend off questions. "Yeah . . . we did think about booking you guys on one of those, but it is quite risky because of unpredictable weather. If a surprise storm blows in, you would be out of luck trying to find a hotel at the last minute. We did not want to take that chance."

The bus slowly rolls into a driveway and drops us off in front of a glittery mini-skyscraper. Pushing through a tall double entrance door, we step into a grand lobby that sparkles with glass, chrome, and ceramic tiles under bright chandeliers. The same spotless, modern look greets me in my spacious room after check-in. It doesn't boast an atmospheric décor as did the room in Huế; still, it is nicely appointed and offers all the comfort that can be expected from a four-star hotel. I open the curtain to a sweeping view of the high-rise-lined avenue which stretches all the way to the bay, where deep-blue outcrops loom dark over the water. With the last vestiges of daylight fast expiring, I grab my camera and snap a few pictures and a video.

Hạ-Long City at sunset.

After unpacking, we gather in the hotel restaurant in the lower level and enjoy a wonderful dinner that features some of the local specialties (seafood soup, calamari, fresh catch). An open market is held nightly near the hotel, so after dinner the more ambitious among us decide to stroll over to check it out, perhaps squeeze in a little bargain hunting while there. Tempted but travel-weary from our long day on the plane and the bus, I opt instead to turn in early.

Hạ-Long Bay is the shortest visit on our itinerary, a mere overnight stay so we can catch a boat cruise in the morning before heading back to Hà-Nội the same day. "There's relatively little to do around here except the bay cruise, and that only takes about four hours," Trí has explained. I've no doubt we could pack our schedule with all sorts of fun activities if given more time, but this being a whirlwind tour with much left to cover still, I get his point. So the next morning we check out after breakfast, then the tour bus drives us to Tuần-Châu Marina on the island of the same name where we'll board our own cruise boat.

Tuần-Châu is one of the larger among the thousands—anywhere between 1,600 and 3,000, depending on sources—of limestone karsts and isles that dot this magnificent bay, the number-one tourist hub in North Việt-Nam. According to local legend, the bay was formed when a giant dragon plunged into the ocean and created the stunning seascape by thrashing its tail, hence the name Hạ-Long, which means "descending dragon." In 1898 a French captain and his crew saw what they claimed looked like giant sea snakes on the bay, and subsequently the news appeared in a French report with the first instance of the name in print.

On the way to the marina, our bus takes a detour through a new development of waterfront condos, estates, and hotels that obviously caters to an exclusive clientele. "See anything unusual about these luxury properties?" says Trí. "They are all unoccupied!" Then, with a chuckle, "The developer is no dummy. He's holding onto them for a while longer for even bigger profits. This is prime real estate here."

The irony can't be missed, of yet another display of capitalism at its rawest in this self-proclaimed communist country. Bold-faced cynicism, or a sign of the times?

We soon arrive at Tuần-Châu Marina, the newest and largest harbor on Hạ-Long Bay and a major port for seaplanes and cruise boats of various sizes. As we step off the bus, I'm struck by the spectacle before my eyes. The huge parking lot looks like the scene outside Disney World, with rows of motor coaches unloading masses of eager-looking tourists who immediately push their way toward the imposing terminal. Many different languages are spoken—shouted— around us, so Trí urges us to insert our earbuds and make sure they're on.

"Yeah, you can see Hạ-Long Bay is a very popular destination," he says, speaking into his wireless mike. "Many of you told me it is on your Bucket List, and as a tour guide I hear that a lot. It was designated a World Heritage Site by UNESCO in 1994 and also made several lists of Best Places to Visit. Most recently, it was voted one of the New Seven Wonders of Nature out of hundreds of candidates from around the world." With such elevated profile, Hạ-Long was chosen to host— at a resort here on Tuần-Châu Island—some later-round activities during the 2008 Miss Universe Pageant. This marked the first time since the end of the war that a major U.S.-based TV program was broadcast from Việt-Nam, also the first time the Miss Universe Pageant was held in a contemporary communist state. Waving his guide's stick like a flag, Trí proceeds toward the crowded terminal. "Let's go find our cruise boat. Follow me close."

We push through the bustle and din of the terminal and spill out onto a long jetty where boats of all different types and sizes are docked. Vending stalls line the quay, and even though it's only mid-morning they're already mobbed with enthusiastic souvenir hunters. But my eyes skip past the booths to the bay beyond, riveted on striking outcrops that surge vertically from the ocean like dorsal fins on a submerged dragon—layer upon layer all the way to the horizon.

Hạ-Long Bay.

With Trí leading the way, we board a modest-sized triple-deck boat halfway down the jetty. As soon as we take our seats in the lower deck, the pilot begins angling the boat out of the busy harbor, at times seemingly racing side by side with other vessels just as anxious to get out in the open water. Once away from the marina, they all disperse across the bay, each tracing its own course among the vast labyrinth of islets. Suddenly the hubbub is gone—nothing but the steady rumble of the boat engine and the sound of lapping waves—and we're surrounded by sea and sky and a dreamscape of unspoiled outcrops towering over the water. Just miles out from the teeming harbor, the boat transports us into another world. A salty breeze blows through the lower deck, sweeping away all travel tension and weariness. I turn my face into the wind and breathe in a deep lungful of sea air. What a heavenly respite this is from the hectic pace we've been keeping.

Trí's voice comes over the earphones, cheerful and excited. "Okay. It looks like we luck out on the weather again. There is no fog, just some high clouds, but they will dissipate later and the sun will come out. Sometimes in bad weather, the fog is so thick you cannot see through it. . . . But isn't it gorgeous around here right now? Why don't we get up on the top deck and enjoy an even better view?" Without further prompting, we grab our jackets and cameras and rush up the narrow stairs to the upper deck, which is roofless and open on all sides.

However many pictures and videos I've seen of Hạ-Long Bay, nothing prepares me for the breathtaking panorama that unfolds around us as we emerge onto the windswept deck. It seems to cast the same effect on the rest of the group since all we can do for a moment is turn and stare in awed silence, until we suddenly come to and start scurrying around in great excitement again. Everywhere we look, unique scenery beckons to be photographed: rock formations of startling shapes and sizes; ever-changing plays of light and shadow behind the sea mist; surprise peek-views through cracks in the limestone pillars; and the multitude of combinations of water, sky, and islets, each one as mesmerizing as the next. We're all dashing from one side of the boat to the other, trying to snap as many pictures as we can of the seascape flowing by, while also pointing out our discoveries to one another. There's so much to take in, no one person can hope to see it all; we're afraid to even blink lest we miss something spectacular.

As Trí moves around and offers to take souvenir photographs for people, he continues to feed us tidbits of information. "Most of the islands here are uninhabited and as pristine as on the day they were formed," he says. "No one knows their exact total number, but at least a thousand of them are large or interesting enough to be given their own names." He goes on to remark that the dramatic shapes of the rocks and pinnacles are being constantly remolded by wind, rain, and waves, as they have been since their earliest beginnings. As a result, one might say that out here on the water the view is never quite the same from one sunrise to the next.

After a while, the initial frenzy begins to die down. Exhilarated but still a bit overwhelmed, we set aside our cameras and video recorders to simply stand and admire the immaculate beauty around us. A hazy sun has peeked through, but the sea breeze is keeping the heat away. Under a brighter sky, the outcrops reveal a fresh green luster from their cover of vegetation.

Peek-a-boo view through a crack.

"It's really something out here, isn't it?" says a man next to me. "Pictures can't do it justice. You just have to be here to experience it. It feels . . . almost mystical." I nod in quiet agreement.

Alone or in groups of two or three, we amble leisurely around the deck to let all our senses soak in the magical environment. I get out my camera for a second round of picture taking, but this time without haste. Then gradually we retreat back down to the bottom deck where the boat owner's wife and daughter have laid out their little display of souvenir wares for sale. We all pick out a few keepsakes to remember this wonderful cruise by, and then, happy and ravenous, we sit down to lunch. It's a simple affair prepared by the same mother-and-daughter team, and the food couldn't be fresher or tastier—the perfect picnic for a fun boat outing. A birthday cake is brought out at the end to help celebrate the happy occasion for two women in the group.

During lunch the boat has drifted to a slow, no-wake speed, and taking advantage of that, a dinghy has appeared from nowhere and accosted it along the side. Loaded with knickknacks and tropical fruit, it's steered by the older of two women in what looks like another mother-daughter team. The daughter leans precariously over the water and reaches up through the boat's opening to peddle their merchandise. A man at my table passes some money to her but doesn't care for anything in return. Ever mindful of our safety and comfort, Trí rushes over and asks the women to move on. Quietly their skiff pulls away. Soon after, our boat also takes off, leaving the little dinghy bobbing in our wake before fading out of sight.

Boats of all types, from mini-cruise ships to ancient-looking sampans with square sails, crisscross the bay. Due to the water's vastness, however, we seldom pass close to any of them. From a distance, they appear like toy boats against the backdrop of sky and limestone ridges, and the wind sometimes carries over the sound of their horns. We thus notice immediately when more than just a handful of vessels begin to circle in the vicinity of our craft.

"Are you guys ready to take more pictures?" asks Trí over his mike. "We are approaching what many consider to be the symbol of Hạ-Long Bay. So come on up to the front with me." As we swarm up around him, cameras at the ready, he goes on, "It's a formation of two big rocks all by themselves, about thirty-five feet tall each. What's special about it is that it takes on totally different shapes depending on which direction you approach from. From here, as we get closer, it will look like a fish jumping out of the water. . . . See the head and the body there? And the smaller tail at the other end?" Aiming the cameras where his finger is pointing, we snap away at the big mass that looms ahead, darkly outlined against the high-noon sun.

The boat glides past the distinctive rock formation a little way then circles around, weaving between other tourist vessels to try and get back close to it from the opposite direction. "This is the best-known view, the one that gives the rocks their name," Trí continues. "From this angle, some people claim they look like a pair of fighting cocks going at each other, but the rest of us see a more romantic image. We say they resemble a pair of fowls leaning their heads together. That's why they are called Hòn Trống Mái, the Rooster and Hen Rocks." At this, the women all go "Aww . . ." and camera shutters go off in a flurry. I suddenly realize that this popular sight, which has become the unofficial logo of Hạ-Long Bay, is actually captured on a piece of embroidery I bought at the workshop the day before. The pretty handicraft now takes on greater meaning as I'm gazing at the real thing with my own eyes.

Hòn Trống Mái (Rooster and Hen Rocks): Emblem of Hạ-Long Bay.

Hạ-Long Bay is also famous for the enchanting *hang* or *động* (caves) scattered all over its islands. Two of the best-known caves are found on Đầu Gỗ (Wooden Head) Island: the "older" and larger Hang

Đầu Gỗ; and the "newer" Động Thiên-Cung (Celestial Palace Grotto), only discovered in 1993 by fishermen taking refuge on the island during a storm. The name Đầu Gỗ dates back to the 13th century when General Trần Hưng Đạo used the cave to hide his wooden stakes with lethal sharp tips. Those stakes were later planted in the estuaries of the nearby Lục-Đầu and Bạch-Đằng Rivers to sink invading Mongol fleets. Since we have just enough time to explore one cave, Trí decides to take our group to Động Thiên-Cung.

Upon approach, Đầu Gỗ Island appears like the perfect setting for an adventure movie: a sheltered small bay at the foot of a sheer cliff covered in flowers and lush vegetation, as pristine as can be if one just overlooks the dock, the crowd, and miscellaneous signage. It brings to mind the legend of Từ Thức, a mandarin in the 14th century who had retired so he would have more time to travel. He was said to have gotten lost at sea during a boat outing—somewhere south of here— and stumbled onto Thiên-Thai, the eternal Land of Bliss. When I mentioned this legend in my book *Once upon a Mulberry Field*, never could I have imagined that one day not too far off I'd find myself in the same environs that had inspired the myth.

Trí has bought tickets in advance, so from the dock we proceed directly up a steep flight of stairs that climbs through trees and rocks to the mouth of the cave, about 80 feet above water. It's not hard to see how the cave had escaped discovery for so long, for the entrance is set back and narrow, well concealed from below. But once we've crossed the hidden threshold, the grotto's 150-yard-long girth opens up before us, a huge hollow under a vaulted dome—the so-called "roof of heaven." Multicolored floodlights illuminate the various odd shapes of stalactites and stalagmites that astound and delight at every step. According to Trí, people have peered at these and claimed they could make out images of Buddha and dragons, as well as flowers, birds, and sea creatures. No matter what they actually look like, I find all these natural sculptures unique and fascinating and scramble to capture as many of them on camera as I can.

The colored lights don't affect me one way or another, but some visitors think they're a bit garish and distracting. "Too much like an amusement park," mumbles a man walking in front of me. The place is bustling with members of other tourist groups, some of whom show little consideration for others as they jostle their way through the crowd while shouting loudly at one another, their voices reverberating throughout the echo chamber. I can only hope they don't cause any damage to this delicate environment by their careless tramping through it. At the end of the winding tunnel, we emerge onto a platform as if from a subterranean world, dazzled as much by bright daylight as by the hidden marvels we've just glimpsed inside.

Stalactites in Động Thiên-Cung (Heavenly Palace Grotto).

From the exit platform, another flight of stairs leads down to the dock. A landing at the midpoint overlooks the bay through a wild growth of bougainvillea, and we all stop here to admire the exquisite view from above and to snap a few last pictures. I suppose Từ Thức must have felt this same tugging inside of him when he said goodbye to the Land of Bliss to return to his native village. We pass by a sign pointing the way to the other cave on the island, the historic Hang Đầu Gỗ, which I wish we had time to explore. But since we're a little behind schedule, Trí is intent on getting us back on the boat and then to Tuần-Châu Marina without further delay.

"I'm sorry for the rush," he says, "but if you really want to see everything, it will take days. There are also many historic sites in the area, but I'm not sure they are of interest to everyone."

I'm aware that this region in North Việt-Nam is steeped in history, going back to the 13th century. Its landscape abounds with monuments that commemorate famous battles and historic figures. Most celebrated among those shrines are the temples at Kiếp-Bạc and Côn Sơn. The first one is dedicated to General Trần Hưng Đạo, who defeated the invincible Mongol hordes not just once but twice (in 1285 and 1287), and the other to the warrior-statesman Nguyễn Trãi, who triumphed over the Chinese Ming army less than 200 years later. Another popular pilgrimage site is the pagoda atop the sacred mountain Yên Tử, about 40 miles northwest of Hạ-Long City. It was there in 1293 when King Trần Nhân Tôn, having presided over the resounding victories against the Mongols, retreated at age 35 to become a monk and the founder of Vietnamese Zen (Thiền Trúc-Lâm). I would love to come back someday, perhaps on my own, to visit those revered places and light incense in tribute to our ancestors and national heroes.

As it is, we immediately board our bus upon returning to the marina, which still looks crowded in mid-afternoon, and are soon on our way back to Hà-Nội, the final stop on our itinerary. After an entire morning at sea, we are now feeling the slow burn of wind and sun on our faces. Pulling the shades closed against the slanting afternoon sun and the chaotic traffic outside, we begin to nod off as the coach bounces along the rough highway.

Some time later, we startle awake when the bus clambers off the road
into the parking lot of the work center where we stopped yesterday.
This is our lone restroom break for the remainder of the ride. Everyone
staggers off the bus to use the facilities, and afterward we wander
through the well-lit shop once more, scanning the vast array of
merchandise to make sure we didn't miss any treasure on the first
go-round. Having admired my embroidered acquisition that depicts
the Rooster and Hen Rocks, a few people set out to find and purchase
the same piece. We then load up on snacks and drinks that will tide
us over until dinnertime and carry them back on the coach with us.
By the time we roll out of the parking lot, ready for the remaining
90-minute drive to Hà-Nội, the sun is already setting.

The break seems to have revitalized the group, and the bus comes
alive with conversations.

Out of the blue, someone asks Trí, "What was it like after the war?"

"Well," he says, "I was born right after the end of the war but
I remember vividly some of those early years." He goes on to explain
that in the '70s and '80s Việt-Nam had to totally rely on aid from the
Soviet Bloc to survive, relations with Red China having deteriorated
to hostile levels. The economy was in tatters, as war had decimated a
couple of generations of young men and severely damaged the country's
already meager infrastructure. In addition, the ruling party had chosen
to adhere to the strictest brand of communism, which only served to
snuff out any remnant spirit or initiative. This, I remember, was
what precipitated the mass exodus of the so-called "boat people"
from Việt-Nam during those years: Having suffered too long and lost
all hope, they risked their lives to escape on flimsy boats in search of
a viable future.

And then the unimaginable happened. By the mid-1980s the Soviet
Union and its satellite states in Eastern Europe were in full disarray,

their systems crumbling much faster than anyone could have anticipated. All aid to Việt-Nam abruptly ceased. That was when, according to Trí, the local regime realized it had to change to survive. Experimental reforms known as Đổi Mới (Renovation) were initiated in 1986 that opened up half of the country—what used to be South Việt-Nam—to international commerce and tourism. The much needed influx of foreign money helped turn the economy around, and the experiment was deemed a great success. The regime waited another 10 years to make sure the new policy posed no threat to its own existence before implementing it in the north as well, in 1996. The rest, as they say, is history.

Listening to Trí, however, I can't help but wonder if he notes the twisted irony in this confusing picture: Why in the world had the regime engaged in bloody warfare for more than 20 years to demolish a system that already existed (in the south), only to go through great pains to rebuild it from the ground up decades after the war had ended—the very system they had so despised? In retrospect, doesn't it all seem an enormous, senseless waste of time, resources, and human lives, to say nothing of the horrific suffering and damage wreaked upon countless innocent people?

Fortunately, I'm rescued from these somber thoughts by the changing scenery outside the windows: We've finally arrived in Hà-Nội. The bus turns off the highway and meanders toward the city center. It's after dark and we're driving through some old business quarters, along small streets lined with trees and semi-dilapidated buildings, their after-hours storefronts shut behind folding steel doors. Trí explains that business buildings get taxed according to the width of their storefronts; that's why most of these, which look like they could predate the war, are narrow and multi-storied. Gnarled bunches of utility cables crisscross over the streets from one end to the other, weaving through trees' foliage like a disaster just waiting to happen. In the faint yellow streetlight, the neighborhood feels like it's still stuck in the waning days of colonialism.

The bus slowly turns a tight corner onto a street that appears to be undergoing a facelift. The left sidewalk looks as forlorn as the sections we just drove through, even with some ramshackle buildings that, if they haven't already been condemned, should be. The right sidewalk is where redevelopment has begun: Half the block was already razed to make space for modern steel-and-glass high rises that tower incongruously over the rest of the street—brightly lit torches in a sea of squalid neglect. One of those new structures is our hotel.

From the outside, it's probably the most modest looking of all the places we've stayed at, a boutique hotel with a stark, narrow façade stretching 10 stories high. A few steps lead up to an unpretentious double glass door that opens in on one side. Filing into the lobby, which sparkles with tiles and mirrors, we stand bunched together while waiting to check in. There is a definite cramped feeling to the place, rendered even more obvious later when I trudge into my compact-sized room. But although not as spacious as other accommodations we've experienced so far, it's still better than adequate, with a cushy double bed and all of the modern comfort one could ask for.

I wait until my luggage is brought up before heading out to dinner. Earlier, Trí has handed each of us a map with directions to a few recommended restaurants downtown. But not feeling like cabbing around the city on my first night here, I stop by the front desk to ask if the staff can suggest a neighborhood eatery within walking distance. They happily oblige and point me to a noodle shop just around the corner which, they assure me, is quite popular with locals.

The sidewalks around the hotel are in worse shape than I thought: very narrow, buckled by tree roots, and riddled with cracks. It wouldn't take much to turn an ankle on such an uneven walk, so I carefully watch my step. The evening air feels muggy, and carried in the warm breeze is a whiff of sewer stench. Around the corner, the street scene becomes more lively as I arrive at a night food market, the type frequented by locals, not tourists. The sidewalk here is strewn with miniature plastic tables and stools that, despite their toy size and sitting low to the ground, seem perfectly comfortable to the customers squatting on them. Following behind other passersby, I slowly pick my way through this obstacle course, which sometimes forces us to go around it by stepping out into the busy street.

Toward the end of the row, I find the noodle shop recommended to me. Like its neighbors, it's no wider than 12 feet across and is so unremarkable in appearance I almost walk right past it, if not for a small sign bearing its name. All the little tables out front are taken, which must be a good sign, so the man at the door waves me inside, where I'm prompted to order and pay. Left to find my own seat, I wander into the crowded space in the back where some nice patrons slide over to make room for me at a long table with low stools. No sooner have I sat down than my food is brought out to me, a steamy bowl of *phở bò* (beef noodles), which I'm familiar with, served with some exotic leaves and fried dough, which I've never seen before. Across from me sit a young mother and her daughter—a little doll, age five or six, with an adorable bob cut. The mother is busy talking on her phone, and it appears the child has been crying, for her cheeks are still damp with tears. When I smile and wink at her, she stops sniffling and snuggles up to her mom's side, from where she watches me with big round eyes through my entire meal.

On the way back to the hotel, I reflect on how curious it is that on one hand I feel so out of place among these people, never having set foot here before, and yet on some deeper level I also sense an instinctive connection with them, with their land and its customs. And then it dawns on me: This is, after all, my parents' hometown, the place where they grew up more than three-quarters of a century ago before migrating south. These tree-lined streets, which probably don't look much different now than they did back then, may well have echoed their young footsteps. In my mind's eye I see them, the smiling youths in old faded black-and-white photographs, strolling past these same narrow storefronts, enjoying a late-night snack at a food market just like this one. With every step, around every street corner, it seems I keep stumbling on missing pieces of the puzzle that was my parents' early lives—a world I knew only through their reminiscence.

Skipping up the steps into the bright hotel lobby, I wonder what other treasures and secrets Hà-Nội will reveal to me over the next two days.

Chapter Five

In the Shadow of History

Saturday, November 12

After a great breakfast at the buffet in the hotel basement, we set out bright and early on a bus tour of the city, which happens to be Trí's hometown. As we ride along the right bank of the Red River (Hồng Hà), just east of the Old Quarter, he points out a long wall covered in ceramic mosaics that runs parallel to the road.

"This wall was built in 2010 to celebrate one thousand years since Hà-Nội was first made the capital of an independent Việt-Nam," he says. "It is three feet high and runs two-and-a-half miles long, and it is recognized in the Guinness Book of Records as the world's largest ceramic mosaic mural. And so this street has become known as Đường Gốm Sứ, or the Ceramic Road." He goes on to explain that the mural is made from ceramic tesserae of Bát Tràng, a village traditionally famous for its brick, tile, and porcelain products. It showcases decorative patterns from different periods of the country's 4000-year history, and also incorporates modern art works as well as children's drawings. "Yeah . . . it was in 1010 that King Lý Thái Tổ moved his capital here. And except for very short periods, Hà-Nội had remained the national capital ever since, up until 1802 when it lost that honor to Huế."

As schoolchildren, we were fascinated to learn that the new capital was originally named Thăng-Long, which means "Ascending Dragon," because the mythical creature was said to have appeared in the sky as

King Lý Thái Tổ was leading the people into the city. It was a great omen for the new dynasty whose founder, the king, had grown up as an orphan monk before becoming a general. In fact, his reign ushered in a long period—over 200 years—of peace and growth for the country. And even though the capital would undergo many name changes throughout history, it would remain fondly remembered as Thăng-Long. In 1831 Emperor Minh-Mạng, ruling from Huế, renamed the city one last time to Hà-Nội, which means "inside the river bend."

Đường Gốm Sứ (Ceramic Road).

The year 1010 marked the establishment of the city as the national capital for the following 800 years, but its history goes back long before that. It was the site of the ancient capital Cổ-Loa (10 miles northeast of the current city center) in the 3rd century BC—when the country was still known by its early name Âu-Lạc—as well as an administrative center during the 1000-year-long Chinese domination that followed. Then in 939 AD, after Ngô Quyền wrested back independence from the Chinese, he symbolically chose the new city near ancient Cổ-Loa as his capital. But after his death, civil war broke out and the capital was relocated to a remote, more defensible site (Hoa-Lư), until King Lý Thái Tổ moved it back to what is now Hà-Nội in 1010.

Closer to our times, in the late 1800s, Việt-Nam fell under French occupation, and the city was made the capital of colonial French Indochina. Then, after the French departed in 1954, Hà-Nội became the capital of communist North Việt-Nam—until 1975 when the North took over the South and the city was proclaimed the capital of the whole country. Today, with a population of eight million and growing, it is the second largest metropolis in Việt-Nam, behind Sài-Gòn.

Already I feel immersed in the long and rich history of the capital, which is intimately tied to that of the entire nation. Names learned long ago from history and literature books are flashing by outside the windows, on street or store signs along our drive. The bus takes us by Trúc-Bạch Lake on the north side of the city. In 1967, U.S. Navy aviator John McCain parachuted wounded into this lake after his airplane was shot down during a bombing mission. He was dragged out of the water and beaten by angry North Vietnamese and was later taken away to the notorious "Hà-Nội Hilton," where he remained prisoner of war until 1973.

Trí waves frantically at a small stone monument on the lakeshore. "Look! Look! That's the 'memorial' dedicated to Senator McCain." We all turn and squint, trying to make out the details on the stone marker. But I've seen pictures of it before and think it would be more accurately described as the "memorial to the capture of John McCain," since it depicts a pilot with his head lowered and his arms raised. The figure is cut off at the knees, giving the impression the pilot is kneeling in a surrendering pose. This, clearly, is a monument to the captors.

Trúc-Bạch is a small lake sectioned off from the larger West Lake (Hồ Tây) by an old dike road named Cổ-Ngư, which in recent years has been widened and assigned a new name. Along this road, on the West Lake shore, stands the city's oldest Buddhist temple: Trấn-Quốc

Pagoda, built in the 6th century AD, where royals had come to worship all through the centuries. The sunset views from its hallowed grounds are known to be breathtaking. Just south of it and a short walk from the John McCain sculpture is the 11th-century Quán Thánh Temple, one of the Four Sacred (Taoist) Temples in the capital. The street that borders the south shores of the lakes is named after the temple, and tucked away somewhere on this street, hidden behind an alley, was the house where my mother and her siblings grew up some 80 years ago. As the bus rolls west on Quán Thánh Street, I recognize most of the names, which my mother had mentioned on occasion with fond nostalgia, and they set my imagination on fire. In my mind, I picture them—my young mother, her sisters and brothers, and their friends, all just coming of age—bike riding or taking a stroll together on Cố-Ngư Road on the weekend; or her and my aunts escorting my grandmother to the pagoda or the temple on holy days to make offerings and pray for blessings for the family. We have no scheduled stop in this area, but luckily I happen to catch a glimpse of Quán Thánh Temple as we drive by, and I manage to snap a fleeting picture of it through the window.

Quán Thánh Temple (11th century) near Trúc-Bạch Lake.

After we've passed the lakes, about five miles west of downtown we arrive at the Museum of Ethnology. Designed in the shape of a bronze drum from the Đông-Sơn culture in the Red River Delta (7th century BC to 3rd century AD), the museum took eight years to build and opened to the public in 1997. It is among the newest and most popular attractions in the capital. Trí leads our group through the exhibit building and out to the park in the back. "Let's go see the garden first," he says, "and then we will come back in here before we leave."

Scattered throughout the well-landscaped grounds are full-scale replicas of housing from 10 of the 54 ethnic groups represented at the museum. We wander through a traditional ranch-style house of the kind found in rural villages in the north—"Almost like the old family house that was passed on to my grandparents," remembers Trí—as well as stilt dwellings and huts with steep-pitched roofs of minorities on the Central Highlands. Along the walk, we stop and watch live demonstrations of such traditional leisure pursuits as water puppetry, classical Vietnamese opera, and calligraphy. You can almost believe you've been transported to a different place and time, if not for those modern high rises looming on the outside over the walls and the trees.

Afterward, we come back into the main building, where we meander through the halls and admire elaborate and colorful exhibits of every-day-life artifacts from the various ethnic groups: costumes, weaving looms, fishing implements, work tools, musical instruments, religious and funerary articles, and a wealth of other functional objects. Trí explains that beyond the outdoor and indoor displays, the museum also maintains a research center, a library, and an auditorium. "I hope this gives you a feel for the ethnic and cultural diversity of our country," he concludes. "You know, there are actually more than fifty-four ethnic groups, but they limited the exhibits to that number because—well, it is deemed a lucky number." He smiles. "Yeah . . . we do believe in things like that. Anyway, it is time we get back to the bus. I still have a lot to show you."

The bus circles back toward downtown to our next stop: the small museum that used to be the gatehouse of the infamous Hoả-Lò (or Stove) Prison. Built in 1886 by the French, the prison was named after the street it was located on, which had a concentration of shops selling wood-fire stoves. But the name quickly evolved to the more baleful meaning, "fiery furnace," when the French used the prison to hold captured Vietnamese nationalists and independence fighters, who were often subject to torture and execution. During the Việt-Nam War, the North Vietnamese kept American prisoners of war at Hoả-Lò—a ploy to deter the U.S. from bombing the capital. For all they endured during their captivity, the POWs sarcastically dubbed the prison the "Hà-Nội Hilton." After the war, it was used to detain political prisoners and dissidents.

Walkway inside Hỏa-Lò Prison (aka the "Hà-Nội Hilton" during the war).

In the 1990s, most of the prison was demolished to free up the prime real estate for a new hotel and commercial complex. Only a small part of it was preserved and later converted into a history museum. One man in our group decides to sit out this tour and waits outside; but the rest of us, intrigued, follow Trí into the museum.

Most of the exhibits show the prison during the French colonial period. Life-sized figures depict half-naked, emaciated prisoners shackled by their legs so they could not stand or walk. Also on display is a horrifying array of chains, whips, and other instruments of torture. Those who dare can check out the tiny solitary confinement cells or sneak a peek at a sinister-looking guillotine in the backroom. The shocking sight of this killing machine suddenly brings back to my mind a history lesson I learned in high school: the failed uprising against the French at Yên-Bái in 1930, following which 13 Vietnamese nationalists, many of them young students and intellectuals, were captured and incarcerated at Hoả-Lò and subsequently condemned to death by the guillotine. Standing just feet from the gruesome apparatus, I feel a spontaneous connection to this tragic chapter in our history, and my eyes well up.

A small section of the museum is devoted to the Việt-Nam War period. The main exhibit is housed in the former interrogation chamber, known to American POWs as the dreaded "blue room" but now presented as a comfortable, albeit spartan, barracks-style room. Besides displays of prisoners' clothes and personal effects, among them John McCain's flight suit and parachute, the exhibit also contains a collection of photographs that contrives to show how well the prisoners supposedly were treated. Such claims have been categorically contested by surviving witnesses in memoirs published after their release from the prison in 1973.

On our way out, we silently pass through a small courtyard shaded by centennial almond trees (*cây bàng*). I gaze up at their lush foliage and wonder, *If only they could talk!*

Hoả-Lò is just blocks away from the city's Old Quarter, which is where the bus deposits us next for our lunch break. In centuries past, artisans congregated in this area along the Red River to ply their trades and cater to the needs of the royal palace. They clustered together by crafts, and over time 36 distinct guilds came into existence, with each occupying its own street. That explains why the street names here begin with the word *hàng*, which means merchandise, with the following word describing the type of product; as an example, Hàng Bạc is the Street of Silversmiths. Even after the French conquered Hà-Nội and tore down many historic parts of the citadel, the Old Quarter continued to thrive and has come to represent the essence of the capital, as summed up in the nostalgic expression, "Hà-Nội of the 36 Streets and the 5 Ancient Gates." Today, with its historic charm and central location, packed with hundreds of quaint shops and restaurants, the Old Quarter is one of the popular tourist attractions in the city.

Trí navigates us through some narrow alleys and gnarled traffic to reach the pedestrian zone at the end of Hàng Trống (Street of Drums). "It's good that we are here on a Saturday," he says. "This nice area around the lake is off limits to traffic on the weekend. It makes it easier for you to explore on foot." He then recommends some lunch places within walking distance and gives us directions to them. "Now go enjoy, but please be sure to return here in two hours. We have a water puppet show to catch. I promise you don't want to miss it."

No longer able to hold back, I dash across the street and arrive on the tree-lined walk along Hồ Hoàn Kiếm, or the famous Lake of the Returned Sword. This is the jewel of the city, located at its heart, the best known and most beloved of all its lakes. When I was a kid, my parents used to have a large black-and-white photo of the lake hanging in our living room; thus its iconic image with the timeless Tháp Rùa (Turtle Tower) reflected in its mirror has long been imprinted on my mind. But what really made the lake unforgettable for me, as a young boy, was the myth that gave rise to its name, a fascinating story that totally captured my imagination.

Tháp Rùa (Turtle Tower) on Hồ Hoàn-Kiếm (Lake of the Returned Sword).

According to legend, in the early 15th century when the country was under Chinese Ming occupation, a resistance leader named Lê Lợi was presented with a magical sword by a golden turtle that lived in the lake, then known as Lục-Thủy (Green Water) Lake. With the help of the sword, Lê Lợi defeated the Chinese after a 10-year struggle and seized back independence for Việt-Nam, establishing himself as Emperor Lê Thái Tổ (1428). One day when the emperor was boating on the lake, the golden turtle emerged from the water again and reclaimed the sword. Since then, this lovely body of water has been called Hồ Hoàn Kiếm, or the Lake of the Returned Sword. In 1886, to commemorate this turning point in the country's history, the Turtle Tower was erected on an islet in the middle of the lake, where an earlier temple had once stood. It has since been cherished by local residents, who consider it the emblem of their city.

For lunch, I decide to try a restaurant on the north end of the lake. Much to my delight, it turns out to be on the third floor of an old building, with a fantastic view of the water. I order the specialty dish the capital is famous for, which was my parents' favorite dish and the same thing that President Obama had (at another restaurant) on his visit to the city back in May 2016: *bún chả* Hà-Nội—or grilled pork patties served on a bed of rice noodles and fresh green vegetables, with a spicy flavored sauce. After a busy and emotional morning, it's pure pleasure to just kick back on the balcony and enjoy a great lunch while watching the crowd beside Hồ Hoàn Kiếm. The weather is agreeable, balmy and overcast but with no rain since the northwest monsoon winter is still a month away, and people are out in droves taking advantage of it.

After putting away my *bún chả*, with time still on my hands, I take a stroll around the lake, starting from the north end where the restaurant is. As I round the corner to head down the east shore, I spot through the trees a red wooden bridge linking the shore to an island with a temple on it. Having seen enough pictures of the bridge before, I immediately recognize it as the other renowned landmark of Hà-Nội: Cầu Thê-Húc, or the Bridge of Condensed Morning Sunlight—don't you love these poetic names—which provides a walking path to the Ngọc-Sơn (or Jade Mountain) Temple on the island. The temple complex, last expanded in 1865, is an architectural gem despite its modest size, and a popular place of worship among locals. This area around the lake has always been a focal point of leisure in the city due to its central location and park-like setting, drawing large crowds of locals and tourists alike, especially on a nice weekend like this one. As I thread my way through the milling throngs, I try to watch ahead and jump out of the way of young newlywed couples or ebullient groups of graduates posing for their pictures by the lakeshore. The atmosphere is wonderfully festive, like at a Fourth-of-July picnic in the U.S.

Famous Cầu Thê-Húc (Bridge of Condensed Morning Sunlight).

Class picture at Hồ Hoàn Kiếm lakeshore.

After reaching the southern tip of the lake, I amble along the west shore and make my way back to our rendezvous point. Trí is already here with some other tour members, waiting for the rest of the group to arrive. When everybody is accounted for, he points to the building right behind us. "In just a minute we will go in there," he says. "It's a theater that specializes in shows of *múa rối nước*, or water puppetry.

I'm excited for you to see this unique Vietnamese art form, almost a thousand years old. The cultural ministry takes it on tours overseas all the time." *Múa rối nước*, we learn, originated from villages in the Red River Delta and used to be performed in flooded rice fields or waist-deep ponds. Puppeteers would stand in the water, hidden behind a bamboo screen, and maneuver the wooden puppets using submerged poles. In modern theaters such as the one we're about to enter, the show is conducted in a water-filled tank on stage.

Heading inside, I'm not sure what to expect, but our show turns out to be quite entertaining from the get-go. It reenacts well-known legends (like the one about the Returned Sword), along with scenes from rural life, with special effects that include fire-breathing dragons, smoke, and firecrackers. Classical *hát chèo* singers dressed in striking costumes sit squatted on one side of the stage, with the traditional orchestra that accompanies them seated on the opposite side. The stories are recounted by the singers, who also lend their mellifluous voices to the puppets. As I watch the lively action unfolding on the water, entranced by the smoke and fireworks and all the novel sounds of ancient music—cymbals, drums, plucking stringed instruments, lyrical voices of *hát chèo* singers—I am struck with awe: So this was how my forebears, even as recent as my grandparents' generation, entertained themselves back in the days (well, perhaps without all the special effects and costumes). What a thrill it is to now be experiencing it for myself.

The show lasts about 45 minutes, and afterward the bus drives us back to the hotel, passing through the former French Quarter in downtown, just southeast of Hoàn Kiếm Lake. I crane my neck and barely catch a glimpse of the elegant façade of the Métropole, Hà-Nội's most storied five-star hotel. Built in the French Neoclassical and Colonial style, the hotel opened in 1901 and has since welcomed a long list of celebrity guests: W. Somerset Maugham, Charlie Chaplin and Paulette Goddard (on their honeymoon), Graham Greene, and Jane Fonda (during her infamous visit in 1972), to name just a few. Having fallen into disrepair during the Việt-Nam War, it was fully restored to its original grandeur in the 1990s and is now considered one of the best hotels in the country. Also fleeting by in short order is the ochre-colored Opera House with its white colonnaded façade and its domed roof and cupolas. Modeled on the Paris Opera House (Palais Garnier), it opened in 1911 and instantly became an architectural landmark of Hà-Nội. But as the bus trundles on, all I can manage is a stolen peek at the majestic building. Shortly after that, to my surprise, we already arrive at the hotel. If I'd had any inkling it was so close to downtown—just over a mile—I would have opted to walk back and taken my time to explore along the way.

Besides the French Quarter, there are some other sites I wish we'd had time to visit. They're all right here in central Hà-Nội, less than two miles west of Hồ Hoàn Kiếm and the Old Quarter, all parts of the ancient capital. Most historic is Hoàng-Thành Thăng-Long, the Imperial Citadel first built in the 11th century under the Lý emperors and subsequently expanded by the Trần, Lê, and Nguyễn dynasties over the course of the millennium.

Đoan-Môn Gate: Entrance to the Imperial Citadel (Hoàng-Thành).

Unfortunately, much of the site was destroyed by the French after their conquest of the city in the late 19th century, but a handful of structures have survived that are historically significant and worth a visit. Lined up on a south-north axis are the 100-foot-tall Flag Tower, the imposing Đoan-Môn (Main Entrance) Gate, the dragon balustrades of Kính-Thiên Palace (the imperial residence), the Princess Pavilion (Hậu-Lâu) behind Kính-Thiên, and the North Gate (Bắc Môn). Despite on-going excavations and restoration projects, the Imperial Citadel has been opened to visitors since late 2004 and was declared a World Heritage Site by UNESCO in 2010.

Just south of the Citadel lies the oldest and the best-preserved architectural complex in Hà-Nội: Văn Miếu, or the Temple of Literature. Initially founded in 1070 to honor the Chinese sage Confucius, it quickly grew to include the Imperial Academy (Quốc Tử Giám), Việt-Nam's first national university (1076). For seven centuries afterward, it continued to serve as the country's foremost center of learning as well as its cultural focal point, until it was supplanted by the new Văn Miếu in Huế, built in 1808 by Emperor Gia-Long of the Nguyễn dynasty.

Graduation ceremony in front of Bái Đường (House of Ceremonies) inside Văn Miếu (Temple of Literature).

The compound's layout was based on the original Temple of Confucius in his birth city of Qufu in Shandong Province, China. It consists of five spacious courtyards populated with elegant buildings, gardens, or pool, and separated from each other by walls and ornamental gateways. As young schoolchildren, we were curious to learn about an age-old tradition that had been initiated at Văn Miếu as a way to honor the nation's best and brightest and encourage learning: Starting in 1484, under Emperor Lê Thánh Tôn, scholars who passed the highest national exam (Tiến-Sĩ) would have their names and the names of their birth villages inscribed on blue-stone steles mounted on giant tortoise pedestals—the tortoise being the symbol of longevity and wisdom. Of the 116 original tablets carrying the names of some 1300 laureates between 1442 and 1779, only 82 tablets survived. This unique collection is mentioned in UNESCO's Memory of the World Program. With such a long and glorious tradition, the Temple of Literature remains to this day a venerable symbol of learning, even to younger generations. I've been told students still stop by the temple to pray for good luck with their exams and to celebrate after graduation. Also, every year before Tết (the Vietnamese New Year), calligraphists in traditional costumes are known to assemble on the pavement around Văn Miếu to write good wishes on lucky-red paper for customers, who buy them to hang around their houses or beside their ancestral altars.

About half a mile west of the Citadel and the Temple of Literature stands the iconic Chùa Một Cột, or One-Pillar Pagoda, modest in size but huge in style and spiritual significance. As with other notable places and monuments in ancient Việt-Nam, the origin of Chùa Một Cột was shrouded in myth. Legend has it that childless Emperor Lý Thái Tôn dreamed that he was visited by the Bodhisattva of Compassion, Quan Âm, who, sitting on a lotus flower, handed him a baby son. Soon after that, the empress indeed became pregnant and bore him an heir. In gratitude, Lý Thái Tôn ordered the construction of a small shrine resting on a single stone pillar in the middle of a pond (1049). Situated in the garden of the larger Diên Hựu (Eternal Blessing) Pagoda, the simple monument was to evoke a lotus blossom rising from a muddy pond, in remembrance of the emperor's dream but also as a Buddhist symbol of purity.

In 1954, as they were retreating from the city, French Foreign Legion forces brought down the temple with explosives, completely destroying it. It has since been reconstructed based on old documents and photographs and now sits in a square-shaped pond, on a concrete pillar 4 feet in diameter and 13 feet tall. The shrine itself is rather small, 10 feet on each side, and is dedicated to Quan Âm. A staircase of stone steps leads up to it from the pool's edge, and tourists and pilgrims alike are said to wait in line to enter it. As kids, we all learned in school about Chùa Một Cột and its special place in our cultural legacy, and even now I can instantly pick it out from any array of photographs with no hesitation whatever. Perhaps for that very reason, in 2012 the Asia Book of Records listed it as one of the most unique works of architecture on the continent.

Chùa Một Cột (One-Pillar Pagoda).

Both the One-Pillar Pagoda and the Temple of Literature are depicted on Vietnamese money bills—the 5,000-*đồng* and the 100,000-*đồng* banknotes, respectively.

With so much history waiting to be discovered around virtually every street corner, history I was taught from textbooks as a child but never had a chance to experience up close, I feel I must plan to return to the city for a much more in-depth exploration. This tour I'm on, I tell myself while getting ready to call it a night, is no more than an introductory sampler.

On our last full day in Hà-Nội, and in Việt-Nam for that matter, Trí brings his nine-year-old son, Tài, to breakfast to meet us. "Babysitting duty today," he explains with a grin. "My wife had to go back to the village early this morning, so he will be stuck with me all day." A bright-looking kid, on the quiet side though by no means timid, the boy makes the rounds of the tables accompanied by his dad, repeating at each stop his formal greeting in excellent English, "It is very nice to meet you. My name is Tài, and I am nine years old."

Trí has planned a day excursion to the city's outlying districts, so after breakfast we ride the bus out to the historic *huyện* Quốc-Oai, a district about 15 miles west of the city center. It used to be part of the former Hà-Tây Province, which was absorbed into the capital in 2008. I've noticed this new trend where the big cities—Sài-Gòn and Hà-Nội—have been swallowing up adjoining territories on their way to becoming giant metropolises. There almost seems to be an obsession with size and growth—bigger is better—and a sense of pride attached to the swelling population count (12 million for Sài-Gòn and 8 million for Hà-Nội, with both capitals still growing).

The moment the bus gets out of downtown and onto the highway heading west, the skyline explodes with modern skyscrapers of great heights. I recall reading in some travel guide that the two tallest buildings in Việt-Nam are located in Hà-Nội, probably not far from where we are, in fact. They went up just a year or two after the Bitexco Financial Tower in Sài-Gòn (the one with the non-rooftop helipad jutting out like a giant disk around its 52nd floor) had claimed that title in 2010. "This is a brand new city over here," says Trí proudly. "Many international companies and businesses have built their offices and factories out in this area. If this was a weekday, we could never move like this. The traffic would be jammed up all along here."

It's a gray day outside, with a sullen sky and a low-hanging fog that renders visibility the worst I've seen on the trip—less than half a mile, is my guess. I ask Trí if this is typical weather for this time of year. "Oh, no, this is not fog," he corrects me. "It is smog from all the factories and traffic. Yeah . . . it gets pretty bad, especially during the week. But it will be even worse in the winter months. That's why most people here don't go anywhere without their face masks." Seeing my shocked expression, the man across the aisle from me shakes his head. "Just like Beijing," he remarks. "Sad, isn't it?" I nod in disbelief, wondering when countries will start to learn from each other's mistakes and recognize that uncontrolled growth at all costs is not without consequences. Hopefully, they'll realize it before it's too late to undo all the damage.

Even without rush-hour traffic, it takes the bus close to 50 minutes to arrive at Chùa Thầy (Master's Pagoda) in Sài-Sơn Village in the Quốc-Oai District. Built in the 10th century, it was expanded 200 years later when the learned monk and Zen master Từ Đạo Hạnh became its abbot. He was said to have invented the art form of water puppetry during his stay here. The pagoda is among the oldest in the country and a popular center of pilgrimage at Tết time.

As we climb off the bus, I'm happy to see that we've escaped from the smog zone. Out here the sky is blue with hardly a cloud, and the bright sun is ratcheting up the temperatures. From the main road, we follow a wide, shady path to the temple, which sits backed up against the Sài-Sơn Mountain, on the south shore of Long Trì, or Dragon Lake.

Chùa Thầy (Master's Pagoda) in Sài-Sơn Village outside Hà-Nội.

A serene courtyard, sheltered by a 700-year-old *cây gạo* tree and decorated with ceramic pots of bonsai and miniature landscapes, fronts the Lower Pagoda. This is the main prayer hall where pilgrims make offerings and ceremonies are held. Anywhere I turn in here, my gaze falls on colorful and lifelike statues of deities and monks in different postures—nearly 100 in total, according to Trí. An open corridor lined with more statues connects the prayer hall to the Middle Pagoda, which sits at a higher elevation and houses a shrine to Buddha. Entering here, visitors are met by two giant and fearsome guardians glaring down from either side of the shrine. They're made of clay and papier-mâché and painted in red lacquer, the largest of their kind in Việt-Nam at 13 feet tall and weighing over a ton each. Across the way from the Middle Pagoda, but sitting yet higher, is the Upper Pagoda, which serves as the worship hall. The most precious statues are kept on the altars in here, of Buddhas and Bodhisattvas and of the three incarnations of Từ Đạo Hạnh—the Master, the King, and the Bodhisattva. A priceless collection of crafts, artworks, and religious articles is also on display, all relics dating back several centuries.

The atmosphere around the temple is light and tranquil; all cares and worries seem to roll off my shoulders the minute I set foot in the ancient courtyard. The place truly invites visitors to slow down and take a moment to clear their minds and souls. I linger in the courtyard for a while longer before rejoining Trí and the group already out by the lake.

Two covered bridges built in the 17th century—the Sun (Nhật-Tiên) and the Moon (Nguyệt-Tiên) Bridges—connect the south shore to an islet on the lake and to a path up the mountain, respectively. Trí waves his hand at a small pavilion rising from the water just off the south shore. "There's the original stage for the water puppet show," he says. "The puppeteers would stand in the back of the pavilion, hidden behind a bamboo curtain just like in the theater. And spectators would gather in front here to watch from the shore." He gives us a big smile. "Hey, if you come back next year in the third lunar month, which is sometime in April, you can catch the show live during the annual festival. Big occasion. Very colorful."

As we wind our way out around the lake, I glance back at Chùa Thầy for one last look and catch the view of the three pagodas with their curved rooflines rising above one another. With its rich legacy and postcard-like surroundings, it's no wonder this place still attracts tourists and pilgrims alike, even after all these centuries.

"Okay. Our next stop will be at So Village, not very far from here," Trí announces as soon as we're all settled in our seats and the bus starts rolling. "It is famous for its traditional product called *miến*, or glass noodle, which is made from arrowroot starch. We will stop and visit with the villagers; that way, you can also observe their daily activities."

Upon arrival just moments later, I'm surprised to find *làng* So to be not at all like my idea of a Vietnamese rural village, typically with dirt roads, bamboo hedges, and mud huts under palm-leaf roofs. Instead, the main village road is paved and dry, and crammed in among old ancestral homes is a new crop of brick houses with tile roofs, many of them with two stories. Regularly spaced utility poles with dangling cables replace the standard bamboo hedge along the road. A few shiny motor scooters lean on their stands in front of houses. Overall, the place exudes an air of prosperity not usually found in a rural hamlet in Southeast Asia. It must be a special model village, one that the government is proud to show off to foreign visitors.

Trí introduces us to a couple of enterprising families who have started their own at-home businesses, and they invite us in to watch them at their work—making "pop rice" (as opposed to popcorn), and knitting head scarves. A small group of giggling children, kindergarten-age boys and girls, scamper after us everywhere we go, apparently as curious about us as we are about them. They readily pose for me to take their pictures and then rush up to my side afterward, eager to view themselves on the camera screen, which in turn renders them giddy with delight.

Trí then takes us to meet an elderly woman in her 80s, one of the last people in the village who still have their black teeth. In ancient Japan and Southeast Asia, it used to be the custom for women to dye their teeth black. This was done for practical reasons since the dye acted as a sealant to help prevent tooth decay. The custom was largely abolished in Việt-Nam in the early 20th century, but it lingered on for a while longer in the countryside. The woman offers us tea and candies, and then, with Trí interpreting for her, she graciously answers our questions about the teeth-dyeing custom. The Q&A session ends with her giving a demonstration on the proper way to chew betel nuts—with mineral lime and wrapped in the leaf of the betel piper vine. These garden products have always been regarded as symbols of matrimony and used as offerings at wedding ceremonies, a tradition that originated from a lovely legend dating back millennia. Before taking leave of our generous hostess, we all gather around her for a souvenir group photo.

On our way back to the bus, we stop to watch a group of village women working diligently to collect sheets of glass noodle being sun dried in the field and load the emptied panels onto carts. From here, the noodle will go back to the factory where it will be sliced up and then sun dried again before being packaged and shipped. Although it doesn't look like really strenuous work at first glance, I have no doubt that the constant up-and-down motion, day in and day out under the scorching sun, makes it backbreaking labor.

Quiet morning at So Village outside Hà-Nội.

From So Village, the bus drives back to Old Quarter in downtown Hà-Nội, where Trí has made a lunch reservation for us at an Italian restaurant. It's a novelty for the locals, especially the younger crowd, but the place also serves traditional Vietnamese dishes, from which I make my selection. The tour is winding down. As exhilarating as it has been, we're all starting to feel the wear and tear from the whirlwind travel, and it shows on all our smiling faces around the table. We have been truly blessed with the weather—little rain, and no excessive heat—but still, most of us are not used to the hot and humid climate of the tropics or to all the dust and smog. As a consequence, some people—myself included, having lived in a different climate zone all these years—have come down with a cough or a sniffle, or even a case of red eyes.

At the end of lunch, Trí makes an announcement: He won't be able to accompany us to the airport in the morning, but a colleague of his will stand in for him and come with us to make sure everything goes without a hitch. "My son and I, we are going back to our village tonight for an important family occasion," he says. "My mother and my wife are already waiting there for us, and tomorrow we will get together with our relatives to rebury my late father." According to this funerary custom called *tảo mộ*, Trí goes on to explain, the remains of the deceased are to be dug up three years after his initial burial, washed, and then reinterred in a nice, permanent plot. All this needs to be carried out in the late fall, but before the winter solstice. Once done, it signifies the official end of the mourning period for the family, and the temporary altar for the deceased can then be moved up to the main ancestral altar. "I'm the only son, so it is my responsibility to take care of all that," says Trí. "But I will still see all of you at our group farewell dinner tonight. Don't forget we leave from the lobby at six-thirty."

Theoretically, we have the afternoon to ourselves, so I've planned to catch a taxicab and do some last-minute touring of my own, perhaps at the ancient Citadel or the Temple of Literature. But since we were late returning from our morning excursion and lunch service has been slow, by the time we finish eating it's already past three. Feeling a little weary and knowing I have a lot of packing to do, I decide to just follow the group back to the hotel.

The afternoon flies by, and I still have things spread out on the bed next to my half-packed suitcase when six-thirty rolls around. We rejoin Trí in the lobby as arranged, and then the bus takes us to our dinner place, a restaurant not far from the Opera House. Despite the prime location, the neighborhood appears dated and shabby, although not as bad as the area around the hotel. Its narrow, deserted streets hardly looks suitable for bus traffic, so we get off the big coach and walk the last couple of blocks to the restaurant, tiptoeing around puddles that smell like stagnant water. The place is not huge, but it is quite popular, packed with foreign customers who, probably like us, have been brought here by their tour guides. The eager owner ushers us to our reserved tables on the second floor, and here we sit down to one of the best meals of the whole trip. There is no really exotic food for us to sample, but every single dish is prepared with just a little extra touch that makes it special—like the delectable mixed rice wrapped in lotus leaf.

Trí makes a toast and we raise our glasses to it. Everyone is already reminiscing about their favorite sights and memorable moments on the tour and sharing pictures and future travel plans. It's beginning to feel like the end. After dinner, satiated and relaxed to the point of languor, we head back to the hotel. I catch one last peek of the illuminated colonnade of the Opera House as we drive past it. In the hotel lobby, we say goodbye to Trí and thank him for having taken such good care of us over the past ten days. Always genial and thoughtful, he has also demonstrated fine organizational skills, with a keen eye for detail. And even though he was born after the war and only knew about it through school teachings, I was interested to learn about his growing up during the turbulent '80s and '90s and how the conditions in Việt-Nam evolved through those final decades of the century. I wish him and his family all the best.

Back to my room, I finish packing then go right to bed since we have to leave early in the morning. During the night, something awakens me. As I toss and turn trying to get back to sleep, the realization hits me full on. How incredible is it that in the past few days I've been able to retrace some of my parents' footsteps, here in their former hometown? I have ridden past the old neighborhoods where they had grown up; walked the same narrow streets they might have walked in the Old Quarter; gazed upon the same city landmarks they had loved and never forgotten; even tasted some of their favorite dishes of Hà-Nội. Together, these fleeting glimpses have opened for me a tiny window on my parents' early lives, those misty years long before any of us kids ever came along. It has given me a rare chance to see them in a wonderful new light: not as loving Mom and Dad, but as two young people just coming of age whom I would have loved to get to know. In the dark of night, the revelation fills me with a sense of wonder and with greater appreciation and love for my parents, who have long been gone.

Morning comes swiftly. After a hasty breakfast, I check out of my room then join our group in the lobby to wait for the ride to the airport. As promised, one of Trí's fellow tour guides has been on hand to help coordinate everything and see to it that all goes smoothly. It's no easy task, considering that we're all catching different flights throughout the day. Some people have left already, and I find out I'm in the next group to go, as soon as the bus gets in from its earlier run. We've barely finished saying goodbye to the remaining people when we see the coach pull up to the front curb. From this point on, everything unfolds quickly and efficiently, as if in fast motion. Soon, the luggage is stowed, we're all on board, and the bus is rolling. Watching the hotel recede from view, I catch a reflection of myself in the window, shaking my head. It is truly over.

Nội-Bài Airport is 20 miles north of downtown Hà-Nội, but with Monday rush-hour traffic, it takes us a good 45 minutes to reach it. The four-story international terminal looks immense and sparkling new, no less impressive than its counterpart in Sài-Gòn. In fact, it took three years to build and has only been in operation since 2015. The inside has the feel of a cavernous hangar, with tall, airy ceilings. Hurried passengers dash back and forth every which way, and long lines are waiting at the counters. Despite the considerable volume of travelers, I detect no serious bottlenecks anywhere as the queues all seem to be moving at a reasonable pace. Our own group gets processed in short order. With ample time on our hands until boarding, we wander the bright corridors lined with restaurants and duty-free shops, until my feet give out and I have to sit down. It doesn't seem real that it was only yesterday we were covering miles on foot without trouble. The sign is clear. As reluctant as I am to admit it, it is time to go home.

But already my mind is feverishly making plans. There's still so much of the country to explore and enjoy, and I can't wait to come back and visit again—for an extended time, at a more relaxed pace, and with my own itinerary of interest. I would love my next trip to Việt-Nam to be more than an introductory tour like this one; I want to make it a real journey of discovery—my personal homecoming. And this time around, I promise myself, I won't have a lifetime of waiting to make up for.

Epilogue

Upon returning from Việt-Nam, I came down with a cold that dragged on for weeks. Although a nuisance, it nevertheless served as a reminder of the unforgiving climate of Southeast Asia—proof positive that I had made it over there and back. For there were times when I woke up in the small hours of the morning, my mind and body still confused from the 15-hour time change, and I wondered if I had not dreamed the entire trip.

Even now, looking back on it, I still shake my head in amazement that it did actually happen, my first visit to my ancestral homeland in 40 years. And what a visit it was, for I got to travel the length of the country and discover it for myself—for the first time in my life. Back during the war, travel had been tightly restricted due to security concerns, and so, growing up, my siblings and I had never ventured far beyond our hometown of Sài-Gòn. Then, when the war ended abruptly in 1975 and sweeping upheaval ensued, I had believed that any real chance to experience our beautiful country had been lost forever. Four decades and much world change later, out of the blue, this whirlwind trip gave me back that opportunity.

A major part of the fun in traveling with a group is to have people to share one's thoughts with, and I often heard my fellow tour members ask one another, "Which place is your favorite so far?" Everyone enjoyed picturesque Hội-An for its intimate setting and fun atmosphere, and Hạ-Long Bay for the breathtaking seascape and natural wonders. The imperial city of Huế, with its scenic mountains and Perfume River and its noble ruins, also ranked high on people's lists. The two contemporary capitals, on the other hand, exerted different kinds of appeal on the tour members: Some found the mix of cosmopolitan modernism and French Colonial charm of Sài-Gòn truly unique and fascinating; others were impressed by Hà-Nội with its thousand-year-old tradition and by the city's transitioning efforts into international metropolis.

When asked if I had a favorite choice of my own, I gave a simple and honest answer: It was every village, town, and city that we had visited, for I would be hard-pressed to pick any one of them over all the others. Having waited for this chance my whole life, I was just thankful to have finally been able to experience these places in person, each in their vibrant uniqueness. Besides, I also felt a natural connection with all of them—as my birthplace or childhood hometown, or my parents' early places of residence, or simply through the shared history and heritage. Whether small hamlet or sprawling city, each gained a special spot in my heart.

A quarter-century after the country had opened its door to the world, commerce appeared to be thriving, especially in urban centers that had remodeled themselves on a grand scale in order to attract foreign tourists. Some resourceful and well-connected young people born after the war had found opportunities in this booming new industry, while other folks—the less privileged and the older—still had to resort to small-scale street vending to survive. I had caught glimpses of the latter just around the corner from luxury hotels and department stores, and had wondered what life was like for them— away from the bright lights of downtown, in a typical rural village and not the model ones we had toured. And so, whenever possible, without detaining the group, I stopped and bought from these street vendors. As I looked into their eyes smiling back at me, the old saying came to my mind: "There, but for the grace of God, go I." It is my hope that the local economy will keep improving, "lifting all boats," including theirs.

But certain things never seem to change. In December, a month after returning home, I saw the news on the internet that the streets of Hội-An were being flooded and tourists had to be evacuated. A related article reported that back in September, just prior to our arrival there, Huế also had been hit by torrential rain that had caused the Perfume River to overflow and inundate the city streets. It was a stark and symbolic reminder of the many challenges the country is still facing; and that, in a blink of an eye, the situation can change dramatically.

I hope with all my heart, however, that the wounds of war will continue to heal—not just from an economic standpoint but in all other aspects as well. Nothing would make me happier than to visit Việt-Nam again in the future and discover each time that more reform and openness have taken root, along with better living and working conditions for all the people. And then one day, hopefully, the rest of the world will find my ancestral homeland as I would love it to be: not a land still saddled with the legacy of war, but a beautiful country and people, with a long and proud history, a rich heritage, and a promising future for all.

Afterword

Thank you so much for reading *Rain Falling on Tamarind Trees*. I hope you enjoyed it. If you have a moment, I would really appreciate a review on Amazon—as short or as long as you wish—to help others decide if they want to give my book a read. Also, if you think it can be of use to someone who is considering a trip to Việt-Nam, please mention the book to her or him.

I'd like to invite you to check out my website at: www.mulberryfieldsforever.com

While you're there, take a minute and browse through my blog posts for more information about Việt-Nam or read an excerpt from my first book, *Once upon a Mulberry Field*, an award-winning novel set in Việt-Nam at the height of the war.

It has been a great pleasure and a privilege to share my trip memories with you. Thank you for your support, and Happy Travel!

About the author:

C. L. Hoàng was born and raised in Việt-Nam during the war and came to the United States in the 1970s. He graduated from the University of California, Berkeley, and earns his living as an electronic engineer, with eleven patents to his name.

CPSIA information can be obtained
at www.ICGtesting.com
Printed in the USA
LVOW06s2039291117
558090LV00037B/319/P